D1331576

The Red in the Rainbow:
Sexuality, Socialism and LGBT Liberation

Hannah Dee

Bookmarks Publications

The Red in the Rainbow: Sexuality, Socialism and LGBT Liberation
Hannah Dee

First published in July 2010 by Bookmarks Publications
c/o 1 Bloomsbury Street, London WC1B 3QE
© Bookmarks Publications

Cover design by Ben Windsor
Typeset by Bookmarks Publications
Printed by Information Press

ISBN 9781905192700

Contents

Acknowledgements

Thank you to Sally Campbell, Mark Harvey, Mary Phillips and Ben Windsor for their help with designing and producing this book. Also to Noel Halifax, Charlie Kimber, Laura Miles, Mark Thomas and Judith Orr who all took the time to give advice and comments, and to Steve Henshall and Dave Sewell for continuing with the daily running of the student office when I was writing the book, occupations and all!

Special thanks to Keith McKenna for his enthusiastic support, thoughtful discussion and detailed work throughout. Also to Viv Smith who helped to conceive the project and discussed closely with me many aspects of the book, and Colin Wilson for very thorough and useful feedback. Finally to my parents Bob and Mal for their endless encouragement and to Jinan, for her support and endurance of many months of obsessive book reading.

Introduction

The modern gay liberation movement was born out of three days of rioting in June 1969 after a police raid on the Stonewall Inn, a gay bar in New York.

At the time homosexuality was treated as a sickness and a crime and those who did the rioting were routinely abused as perverted and mentally ill. But they took inspiration from the mass anti-war, civil rights and black power movements raging in the US. Chanting "Gay power", they called for a revolution to realise "complete sexual liberation" and started a mass movement that was to change the lives of lesbian, gay, bisexual and transgender (LGBT) people forever.

LGBT liberation has come a long way since then. In the last two decades alone we have seen a wave of legislative changes in favour of gay rights. Attitudes have shifted – a recent poll found 90 percent of people in Britain supportive of gay rights, while only 20 years ago 70 percent of the British public thought homosexuality was "always or mostly wrong". Today LGBT people are a more visible and confident part of society. The simple act of holding hands in public would have been risked by few in the 1960s.

Despite these immense changes Britain can still be a dangerous place for LGBT people. In 2005 a young gay man, Jody Dobrowski, was beaten to death so violently that his family could not identify him. A string of other brutal murders have since taken place and in the last year there has been a shocking increase in reported homophobic attacks across a number of major cities.

Hate crimes are not the only problem. In the 1970s the

gay movement called for a challenge to the pattern of institutional oppression across all the major institutions in society: in schools, the church, the media, employment, psychiatry and mental health. Today that systematic discrimination persists. How else to characterise the pitiful 1 percent conviction rate for reported homophobic attacks? Or the refusal of the majority of schools to organise anti-bullying policies despite the abuse faced by young LGBT people, leaving them six times more likely to commit suicide than their peers?

The return of the Tories to government in 2010 – the party responsible for Section 28, a law which banned discussion of gay sexuality in our schools unless in the context of death or disease – has also generated anger and fear that the clocks could be turned back. These fears have been confirmed by a series of bigoted outbursts by Tory politicians who have supported the "rights" of B&B owners to ban gay guests, compared the "danger" of gay sex to being in the army and declared that gays are not "normal".

So is this as good as it gets? What can we do to defend what we have? Is it still possible to fight for the kind of change the Stonewall rioters demanded – "new forms and relations...based upon brotherhood, cooperation, human love and uninhibited sexuality"?

Socialists have something important to say in response to these questions.

For too long official LGBT politics has been confined to talking about equality and organising to achieve legal reforms. This work is important. No one wants to go back to the 1960s, when sex between men was a crime, or the 1980s, when AIDS was dubbed a "gay plague" by politicians and the media, fuelling a massive increase in the persecution of LGBT people. But the persistence of oppression in all walks of life shows that despite our achievements in changing the law, it is no guarantee against discrimination.

We have seen also the commercialisation of the gay scene

and our sexual identity to the point that London Pride – once a militant demonstration in commemoration of the Stonewall riots – has become a corporate-sponsored event far removed from any challenge to the ongoing injustices we face. In 2007 it was led by the police and the Royal Navy – sections of the establishment that are implicated in the oppression of LGBT and other people here and around the world.

And herein lies the problem. LGBT oppression persists precisely because despite the gains we have made, it is rooted in the wider organisation of capitalist society. In a system driven by exploitation and competition those in power must subject every aspect of our lives – even our personal relationships – to the priorities of profit-making. This has shaped the institution of the family, which plays a vital role in regulating such relationships and is a key mechanism for reproducing both the class that rules and a workforce on the cheap. Politicians, big business and the media eulogise about family values while heaping huge burdens on ordinary people to carry out everything from childcare to looking after the sick and the elderly in the home, for free. Meanwhile LGBT people are seen as a problem because we undermine and disrupt the relationships and roles that the traditional family rests on. To allow us to express our sexuality or gender identity freely would be to question the whole basis of the family and begin to undermine some of the prejudices and divisions that are used to keep the system going.

That is why, if we are going to achieve a genuine and lasting liberation, we need to be part of a wider struggle to change the world.

The experience of LGBT struggles bears this out. The gay liberation movement of the 1960s and 1970s was able to win so much because it was part of a larger revolt against the system. In country after country the oppressed and exploited rose up to challenge the ruling class; mass strikes shut down whole economies, governments were brought to their knees, and another world seemed possible. In the end that world was not born, but the scale of resistance forced those in power to concede reforms, and lasting gains for LGBT people and other oppressed groups were won.

This link between LGBT struggle and wider social revolt runs through the history of our fight for sexual liberation like the red in the rainbow. Socialists and the working class movement have been central to that history.

So when governments were first introducing laws to criminalise gay men in the late 19th century it was individuals and movements connected to working class and socialist organisations that fought back. In England the gay rights pioneer Edward Carpenter spent his life agitating inside the working class movement for a socialist society which would see "love's coming of age" at a time when a huge moral panic was being mobilised against men of the "Oscar Wilde sort". In Germany the largest working class party in the world, the German Social Democratic Party, played a central role in the campaign against anti-gay laws, and was the only party to oppose them in the German parliament. A revolution in Russia saw a new workers' democracy abolish anti-gay laws and introduce a raft of reforms aimed at liberating people's lives and sexual relationships from the old ways. The age of consent was abolished, divorce on demand was introduced, abortion legalised and "the absolute non-involvement of state and society in sexual relations" declared.

One reason why this radical history is largely hidden is because many of those early movements were defeated. In Russia the hopes of building a new society that would achieve liberation for all were defeated by the rise of Stalin. In Germany the vibrant gay movement and subculture was brutally crushed by the rise of Hitler and the Nazis. Millions were murdered: gays, Jews, trade unionists, socialists, and along with them the memory of workers' resistance and revolution as the "festival of the oppressed".

But it is a tradition that has continued to prove central in resisting attacks against LGBT people and winning the gains we enjoy today. When Thatcher and the Tories attempted to roll back LGBT rights in the 1980s, widespread support in the trade union movement – from the miners who led Gay Pride in 1985 to the teachers who marched against Section 28 – was crucial to stopping them. In the following decade a mass movement in South Africa overthrew the racist apartheid regime and it became the first country to enshrine LGBT rights in its constitution.

It is time to renew this radical struggle for a sexual liberation where we are free to express who we are, and love who we want, without fear, legal persecution or commercial exploitation. It is time to rediscover the red in the rainbow.

A note on language

The fight for sexual liberation has always involved a struggle by the oppressed to develop a language that asserts our sexuality or gender identity with pride against a society which not only discriminates against us, but denigrates us with abusive words. During the 1960s, for example, the slogans "Gay is good" and "Gay and proud" were an important element in a wider struggle against a society which attacked us for being "queers" and "perverts". Because this book is a history of such struggles, the terms used will change at different points – from homosexual, to gay and lesbian, to LGBT – to reflect the language most commonly used at the particular historical period being discussed, by those doing the oppressing, and those fighting back. When it comes to looking at current day society and struggle I will use LGBT to refer collectively to all those oppressed because of their gender identity or sexuality as the most common political term used by those involved in resisting oppression since the early 1990s. Some people claim this term still leaves out groups of people who are oppressed and prefer to opt for the terms Queer or LGBTQ. While I share the desire to build a struggle which can bring together the widest possible numbers of people in a common cause against sexual and gender oppression, I also think the word Queer can be a barrier to such a project since for the vast majority of people it remains a cruel term of abuse. I hope, however, we can continue to debate these questions in the movement as we unite to fight for a future world that embraces everyone regardless of their sexuality or gender identity. For more discussion of language and Queer politics see pages 129-135.

1: A history of the "beautiful love"

One of the biggest questions confronting anyone involved in the struggle to win a world where we can all be free, regardless of our sexuality or gender identity, is where does LGBT oppression come from? Why is it that people are persecuted and discriminated against because of who they desire or love, or because of how they choose to define their gender? Where do these categories of gay, straight, lesbian, bisexual and trans come from? And why do we have to use them to label our most intimate desires and emotions as if they are facts to be categorised not things to be felt, explored and expressed freely?

Of course it is important that in a world where sexual oppression exists growing numbers of people are choosing to come out and assert they are L, G, B or T with pride. This is a small act of resistance that can be a step towards challenging prejudices, standing up to discrimination and demanding we are treated with respect. But it doesn't end the oppression we will face, perhaps for the rest of our lives, and this is why many people will choose to stay in the closet fearing a range of consequences from family rejection to physical attack. So how has it come to this?

The bigots' answer is simple – LGBT people are trying to go against the natural order of things. Heterosexuality is normal, the argument goes, because it can lead to the reproduction of children; homosexuality is not. But most straight people depend on some form of contraception to have pleasurable sex lives, and human sexuality is far too varied and complex to be divided into two boxes.

It is suggested that in Britain around 6 percent[1] of the population define themselves as lesbian, gay or bisexual, yet numerous polls show that up to twice that proportion have experienced either desire for, or sexual intimacy with, someone of the same sex.[2] A similar poll in New Zealand found that 20 percent of people reported having experienced some "homosexual" feelings but only 2 to 3 percent defined themselves as lesbian, gay or bisexual.[3] The prevalence of same-sex activity and desires among the population at large, including those who define themselves as heterosexual, has been confirmed by numerous studies since the famous "Kinsey Reports" of 1948 and 1953 – the first major research into sexuality carried out by Alfred Kinsey, the founder of the American Institute for Sexual Studies. These showed that 50 percent of men and 28 percent of women who took part in the research had experienced sexual desire for members of their own sex, and 37 percent of men and 13 percent of women had experienced gay or lesbian sex.[4] Kinsey concluded that "such activity would appear in the histories of a much larger proportion of the population if there were no social restraints"[5] and that:

Only the human mind invents categories and tries to force facts into separated pigeonholes. The living world is a continuum in each and every one of its aspects. The sooner we learn this concerning human sexual behaviour, the sooner we shall reach a sound understanding of the realities of sex.[6]

Kinsey's research dealt with sexual behaviour. But we must also consider people's desires, how they think of themselves and how others think of them. The connections between these different aspects of people's lives can be complex, and are shaped by the wider social context in which people live. As Colin Wilson argues:

Being gay or straight is not just about having sex with men or women or both, but about the whole circumstances of one's

THE RED IN THE RAINBOW

life. For example, many men who go "cottaging" – looking for sex in public toilets – are married. Are such men gay? What if such a man lives with his wife and children? What if everyone thinks of him as straight? What if he thinks of himself as straight? What about a woman who leaves her husband to live with another woman? Has she really been a lesbian all along, even if she has never been attracted to women before? The idea that people divide up simply between gay and straight is far too simplistic.[7]

This is not to say that no one is exclusively heterosexual or gay or lesbian or that everybody is bisexual. (Kinsey, for example, proposed a scale ranging from 0 to 6 to describe people's sexual behaviour and histories, where 0 is exclusively heterosexual and 6 exclusively homosexual.) But it does mean that the simple categories of gay and straight do not accurately describe the complexity of many people's lives, and that the oppression and persecution of LGBT people acts to constrain the freedom all people have to express their sexuality.

We cannot know what human sexuality might look like in a society that doesn't seek to cage our relationships in a narrow set of prejudices, conventions and taboos. But we can look at what has come before.

Same-sex love, desire and relationships, as well as gender variance, are as old as humanity itself. They have occurred throughout human history, across large parts of the world, within a wide range of different societies and cultures. But the labels and ideas we attach to them today are little over 100 years old. The term "homosexual" was first coined in 1869 and those of lesbian, bisexual, trans and heterosexual followed later. Prior to this people enjoyed same-sex relations and close emotional relationships without ever thinking of themselves as a separate category of person and without being named as such.

There is also no evidence that the systematic oppression of LGBT people existed until very recently. Certain forms of sexual activity have been restricted and punished in some societies, but it was the acts which were criminalised, not a category of people. This is not to take away from the pain and sometimes horror inflicted on people "caught in the act", but the punishment of a wide range of sexual acts is of quite a different order to the uniform and systematic persecution of what society has come to distinguish as a type of person, be it gay, lesbian or bisexual.

So across the huge span of different human societies we can find many examples of same-sex relations being accepted and integrated into everyday life and in some cases revered and celebrated. In the earliest human societies, for example, cross-gender transfer was common among the indigenous people of the Americas. A man or woman who showed a preference for the activities of the opposite sex could be initiated into that gender. They would then carry out economic and social duties according to their acquired gender, including sexual relations and marriage with members of the same sex. European colonialists observed in North America "a man who was married to another…[man who was] clothed and attired like a woman, and perform[ing] the office of a woman",[8] and noted that such people were highly valued in their communities. Referred to today as "two spirit" people, similar practices existed among the pre-colonial civilisations of Latin America – the Aztecs, Mayans, Quechuas, Moches, Zapotecas and Tupinamba. They have also been found across a wide range of African societies including the Iteso people in Kenya and Uganda, the Konso of Ethiopia and the Ashanti of West Africa.[9]

There is a wealth of literature and cultural artefacts from ancient Greece and Rome that are testament to a celebration of love between members of the male sex. The philosopher Plato refers to male love in his philosophical text *Symposium* as "the beautiful love" and "heavenly love" as opposed to "common love" between men and women. An anonymous poet in ancient Rome observed, "One person likes one, another likes the other, I like both".[10]

Similar sentiments are to be found in Islamic art, literature, folk tales and poetry, reflecting a situation in which same-sex desire was a common part of life across large areas of the Middle East and North Africa before colonisation. There are numerous references to it in *One Thousand and One Nights*, a tapestry of stories drawn from the region between the 8th and 15th centuries. When Europeans encountered these practices in the countries they occupied in the 19th century they were quick to condemn them in word and law. At the same time many individual Europeans were only too happy to escape the more repressive environments of their own countries. As the French novelist Gustave Flaubert put it while travelling in Egypt, "Here it's quite well accepted. One admits one's sodomy and talks about it at the dinner table."

This historical and cultural evidence of variation in sexual practices, relationships and attitudes is important because it shows that LGBT oppression is not an inevitable, timeless feature of human society.

It also goes some way towards challenging the common-sense notions about where this oppression comes from. The claim that LGBT oppression is a result of human nature or natural prejudice, for example, cannot explain the fact that a wide range of human societies have embraced same-sex relationships or gender variance in the past. The suggestion that religion is the cause is similarly undermined by the widespread acceptance of love between men in the work of respected Islamic scholars, poets and writers spanning centuries in the Middle East.[11] There is also evidence of a more complex set of attitudes towards male and female relationships in Christianity than one might expect. There is, for example, the survival of religious tombs dating from the Middle Ages in which two men, and sometimes two women, are buried together as if man and wife. Documentation from the same period also refers to ceremonies which formally recognised intimate emotional relationships between men in the same period.[12]

Neither can the view that human sexuality is reducible to a set of given biological facts, determined by "gay brains" or "gay genes", explain the widespread existence of different kinds of relationships, both same-sex and between opposite sexes.

This does not mean that people in such societies enjoyed complete sexual freedom. Often there were strict rules and regulations about what was permissible and certain sexual acts were heavily persecuted.

Greece and Rome were built on slavery and were extremely oppressive towards women, which is why we know very little about erotic relationships between women in those societies. In the ancient Greek city of Athens male sex with teenage boys was acceptable, but only if it did not challenge the gender roles and hierarchies on which that society was based. There had to be a suitable age gap between the "active" man and "passive" boy, for example, with any reversal of such roles being considered obscene. In Imperial Rome it was acceptable to rape slaves, because they were considered the property of "freemen", yet it was not permissible for the free-man to willingly consent to a slave. As one lawyer put it, "Sexual service is an offence for the freeborn, a necessity for the slave and a duty for the freedman".[13]

How then do we make sense of the wide range of sexual practices and attitudes towards sexuality? What shapes, and who makes, the seemingly arbitrary rules about what is or is not acceptable? And why at a certain point in history did that lead to a new set of categories for people with a particular sexual orientation, followed by the systematic oppression of LGBT people?

For Marxists the key to understanding how people's attitudes to sexuality, gender and sex are formed, and how they decide what is "normal" in a given society, lies in our understanding of the family as an institution rooted in class societies – both capitalist and earlier forms.

Today those who attack gay sexuality often do so on the basis that our choices and relationships threaten the "traditional family", ie men and women getting together, settling down and having children. Of course a lot of people, not just LGBT people, choose not to live in this way while some lesbians and gays choose to form families of their own. But the "traditional family" remains a very powerful institution that structures our lives and the ideology of our society. It is continually promoted and reinforced through laws, by politicians, in the media and across a range of institutions in a way that systematically undermines and marginalises LGBT people. A recent pilot of a school book, *And Tango Makes Three*, about two male penguins who fall in love, hatch a baby penguin from an egg and raise the chick as their own, was met with outrage by some people precisely because it would suggest to young children that same-sex couples could be compared to traditional family relationships.

The family has played an important role in shaping and enforcing sexual conformity and gender roles across a range of societies. In order to understand how and why this happens it is necessary to look at its roots in the development of class society and the role it has played in maintaining class power.

Engels – revolutionising the way we see the world

One of the most important books on this subject is Frederick Engels's *The Origin of the Family, Private Property and the State*. It was written in 1880s Victorian Britain – the same decade that new laws were introduced which criminalised homosexual men for the first time. These laws were part of a wider drive by the British capitalist class to consolidate its power at home and extend it to other parts of the world. At home authority was shored up by strengthening the family and promoting an ideology that naturalised women's place in the home and attacked any sexual variation outside the family. The colonisation of other countries was supported through racism. Gender, race and sexuality, even the poor, became categories ordered into hierarchies to justify oppression and exploitation as the natural order of things.

Engels completely challenged this view of the world. He drew on anthropological studies of societies from America to the Mediterranean to show that the systematic oppression of women, the existence of the nuclear family and even nation-states were relatively recent developments. He not only attacked the sacred institutions of Victorian society, he called for a revolution to overthrow them – a "festival of the oppressed" which would end the rule of one class over another, and liberate women and sexuality.

Engels's work remains highly valuable in providing us with a framework for locating the roots of sexual oppression in the wider organisation of society. As Engels put it:

According to the materialist conception, the determining factor in history is, in the final instance, the production and reproduction of immediate life...on the one side, the production of the means of existence, of food, clothing and shelter and the tools necessary for production; on the other side the production of human beings themselves, the propagation of the species. The social institutions under which men of a definite epoch and definite country live are conditioned by both types of production.[14]

The core argument laid out in *The Origin of the Family,*

Private Property and the State has been supported by many other studies since. There are, however, details in his account that reflect the weaknesses of some of his sources at the time and contain some speculation which cannot be proved either way.

Our knowledge about previous societies will always be partial and its interpretation shaped by modern prejudices. Some of our major sources of information about the earliest human societies, for example, come from colonialists and missionaries whose accounts are clearly distorted by their own assumptions and narrow-mindedness. The existence of women's oppression means that we have much less information about same-sex relationships between women than we do about men, and in both cases it is the sexual lives of the wealthy classes that we know the most about.

Nevertheless, there is plenty of evidence to show that human beings have lived in a large variety of ways, and that class society has existed for only a tiny proportion, perhaps 7-8,000 of the 100,000 years or so that biologically modern humans have inhabited the planet. We also know that the corollary of more equal economic relationships that existed before class divisions arose was much freer relationships between men and women with fewer restrictions on sexuality.

In hunter-gatherer societies, for example, where the "two spirits" were known, people lived a nomadic existence, moving around at regular intervals in search of new sources of food. People were dependent on each other – they feasted or starved together – and the values of sharing, solidarity, equality and generosity flowed from this.

The lack of any surplus food or wealth meant that there was no material basis for a ruling class or authority. Missionaries writing in the 1600s about the Montagnais-Naskapi of Canada, who they were attempting to "civilise", complained:

Alas if someone could stop the wanderings of the savages and give authority to one of them, we could see them converted and civilised in a short time...they have neither political organisation, nor office, nor dignities...as they are contented with a mere living, not one of them gives himself to the Devil to acquire wealth.[15]

There was a sexual division of labour in which, by and large, the women did the gathering and the men did the hunting. This was mainly because it was not easy to combine pregnancy and breastfeeding young children with activities such as hunting. But there was no hierarchy or value judgement attached to these roles. Hunting could bring the most highly prized food, but gathering was the most reliable and regular source of food. So among the Montagnais, the women were said to "have great power" and "in nearly every instance...the choice of undertakings of journeys and winterings" lay in their hands.

Women's role in reproduction did not stop them from playing a full role in the tribe, nor was childcare seen as the main responsibility of women. A missionary preaching about the sexual independence of Montagnais women, for example, records the riposte he received from one of the tribesmen:

I told him that it was not honourable for a woman to love anyone else except her husband and that this evil, being among them, he himself was not sure that his son, who was there present, was his son... The man replied thou hast no sense. You French people love only your own children, but we love all the children of our tribe.[16]

So children were seen as a collective responsibility, rather than the personal responsibilities or even properties of particular women or families. Because people were linked together through relationships of mutual interdependence it made no sense for people to divide up into separate nuclear families with individualised duties. As a consequence, men and women also enjoyed a high level of sexual autonomy in which sexual relationships were not tied into immediate family responsibilities or moral obligations. It was reported:

> The young people among the Montagnais do not think they can persevere in the state of matrimony with a bad wife or a bad husband… They wish to be free and to be able to divorce the consort if they do not love each other. The inconstancy of marriages and the frequency with which they divorce each other, are a great obstacle to the Faith of Jesus Christ. We do not dare baptise the young people because experience teaches us that the custom of abandoning a disagreeable wife or husband has a strong hold on them.[17]

The absence of any systematic classification of people on the basis of their gender, or restrictive moral codes regarding sexual relationships, perhaps explains the acceptance of two-spirit people within some hunter-gatherer societies. If the economic contribution of men and women is equally valued, and there exist no fixed ideas about the sexual or social behaviour or characteristics attributed to the gender of a person, then crossing between genders presents no problems.

Yet the colonisers who came across them treated them with horror. The two-spirit people among the Karankawa Indians in Texas were described by the Spanish colonisers in the 1500s as "the most brutish and beastly custom to wit".[18] When they were talked about in the colonising countries, they were referred to as "berdaches" – implying male prostitute, catamite or sodomite.

So what changed?

How did we get from the relative sexual freedom of the hunter-gatherers to the strict moral code and repressive attitude of the colonisers?

A crucial shift took place around 10,000 years ago with the beginning of agricultural societies, when some groups began combining hunting and gathering with the cultivation of crops and keeping animal stock. One consequence of this was the production of a surplus that could be stored and kept for hard times.

Producing a surplus gave rise to a layer of people whose primary role was to protect and administer it. A division formed between those who were directly producing and those with control over the surplus. This crystallised into a class structure in which those controlling the surplus developed methods for maintaining that structure. These were to include, crucially, the bodies of armed men which form the basis of the state and a reshaping of other institutions such as the family.

This was not some smooth, uniform process, but took place in different ways over thousands of years. The exact route through which societies developed from hunter gathering to civilisation also varied significantly. The earliest civilisations in Mesopotamia, Egypt, Iran, the Indus Valley and China arose through a process of internal development but most were forced to change by military conquest, colonisation and trade including northern Europe. Nevertheless the general trends by which class divisions develop are shared across those societies.[19]

The rise of an exploiting class, and women's oppression, was not caused by human greed or male chauvinism but rooted in a situation of real scarcity. The developing division between those producing the resources and those controlling them was initially a way to help protect, allocate and propel forward the overall resources in society. But it gave a small minority privileged access to those resources, undermining the egalitarian ways of living that had gone before. From this developed new structures of power and a distinct class that could exploit and divert wealth away from the majority in society.

The changes in production had a profound impact on the role of women in society. A bigger population was required to provide workers in the fields. Women who were frequently pregnant or breastfeeding could not so easily participate in the heavy labour required by new production techniques, such as the plough and the construction of irrigation systems. Gradually women's once central role in production and public life was reduced to the demands of reproduction. Men became increasingly central to the activity which produced a surplus.

This undermined the interdependent relationship between men and women that had formed the basis of equality between the sexes. As class divisions developed, men's economic role in production gave them a privileged position in the household. Societies where the children were cared for collectively had to be changed as this threatened multiple claims on the wealth of the new ruling class. They required instead a privatised family based on the strict monogamy of the woman, who was to produce children whose paternity, and therefore rights to inherit wealth, could be guaranteed. But doing this also meant that the woman, and her sexuality, had to be strictly controlled, both physically and ideologically:

Among the remains of prehistoric societies...female statuettes abound suggesting the worship of goddesses, while phallic statues are lacking. Once class societies develop the stress is increasingly on the role of gods, with the great religions which dominated from the 5th century BC onwards across the most of Eurasia characterised by the omnipotence of a single male god. The ideology of both rulers and ruled became one of male dominance, even if female figures were sometimes allowed a subordinate role.[20]

Engels argued:

> The overthrow of the mother right was the world historic defeat of the female sex. The man took command in the home also; the woman was degraded and reduced to servitude; she became the slave of his lust and a mere instrument for the production of children... In order to make certain the wife's fidelity and therefore the paternity of his children, she was delivered over unconditionally into the power of the husband; if he kills her, he is only exercising his rights.[21]

So while wealth and wellbeing was increasing in society, this was at the cost of the majority of people losing control over what they produced. In this sense it was also a defeat for the majority of men.

Different class societies were to define the family and what was sexually permissible according to the demands of property relations. This process was barely concealed under the ancient Roman Empire where the family was an essential fortress for the protection of ruling class wealth. Engels pointed out:

> The original meaning of the word family (*familia*) is not the compound of sentimentality and domestic strife which forms the ideal of the present-day philistine; among the Romans it did not at first even refer to the married pair and their children but only to their slaves. *Famulus* means domestic slave, and *familia* is the total number of slaves belonging to one man. As late as the time of Gaius, the [inheritance] was bequeathed by will. The term was invented by the Romans to

denote a new social organism whose head ruled over wife and children and a number of slaves and was invested under Roman paternal power with rights of life and death over all of them.[22]

Women were formally denied any sexual autonomy, whereas ruling men could seek a number of objects of pleasure, from the slave to the freedman to the prostitute. It has been suggested that the flexibility towards same-sex relations stemmed from the fact that the ancient Greek and Roman economies were built on the conquest of slave labour. Reproduction of a working population was not central to creating the wealth of the ruling class, so there was no great need to be restrictive about non-procreative sex outside the family. At the same time the family, and the restriction of women's sexuality, was necessary for the protection of wealth. As one Greek orator put it, "We keep mistresses for the sake of pleasure, concubines for the daily care of our persons, but wives to bear us legitimate children and to be faithful guardians of our households".[23]

So what underlies a set of codes governing sexual behaviour and gender roles across a range of class societies are the institutions of private property and the family: same-sex relations are allowed insofar as they do not challenge these institutions.

Li Yu's 17th century Chinese play *Pitying the Perfumed Companion*, for example, tells the true story of a married woman who falls in love with another woman. Despairing that they have to separate she eventually pleads with her husband to take on her lover as a concubine. He agrees and "the play ends happily".[24]

The range of what is permissible is always shaped by the material, social and political conditions in society. The feudal system in Europe depended on serfs rather than slaves. Serfs had some access to land and could produce their own food, but they were far from free. There were many restrictions on their lives, including their right to move about the country. Although they were free to marry and have children, these children were expected to carry out future labour and military service for their lord. In these circumstances a quite different set of controls on sexuality developed. The highly visible, even celebrated sexual relationships between men that had occurred in ancient Greek and Roman civilisations would undermine a set of ideas that stressed the moral obligation to reproduce within the family. New restrictions that strengthened marriage and punished the "heavenly love" had already been introduced by a succession of Roman rulers trying to shore up their crumbling empire, as it was deprived of fresh labour through conquest.

This sharpening persecution of non-reproductive sex was reflected in Christianity, which went from being a marginal faith to the official religion of the Roman Empire at the turn of the 5th century. The religion combined a stress on the duty of men and women to reproduce within wedlock with an attack on supposed "sins against nature", a catalogue of non-procreative sexual acts, ranging from masturbation and bestiality to anal sex, which it was claimed would bring all kinds of disasters from plagues to famine onto the population. Christianity was able to act as an ideological cement for the new ruling class:

> It appeared as a spiritual, theological and magical explanation in which the Roman gods had failed to save the state but the Christian god would save the individual who supported the Christian clergy, took regular part in their rituals, and observed the rules of Christian sexual morality. The masses as well as the rulers turned to it as the heart in a heartless world, and a way of making sense of the world they lived in.[25]

It would be a mistake to root the causes of modern-day LGBT oppression in the rise of Christianity or any other religion. The targets of the Christian establishment through the Middle Ages didn't involve any notion of the homosexual or lesbian, nor did they single out same-sex activity as a special threat, over and above other "unnatural crimes" such as adultery. These acts of "sodomy" were not even seen as sexual crimes in the modern sense, but were associated with a reversal of the order of nature, and therefore with religious heresy and treachery to one's king or lord.

What is clear is that when those in power felt threatened they mobilised attacks on proscribed sexual activities and other scapegoats such as heretics, Jews and witches. So the increased persecution of "unnatural crimes" at different points from the 13th century onwards can be related to the way in which economic developments were undermining the stability of traditional institutions.

Henry VIII's 1533 Buggery Act, which carried the death sentence for those who committed sodomy (women with men, men with men and men with animals) should be seen as part of this wider fight for social control. In England marriage laws were formalised and the crime of sodomy was included in the Articles of War – putting it on a level with mutiny and treason. The application of the death sentence for sodomy was not repealed until 1861 and various buggery laws continued to be used to criminalise and imprison gay men until 1967. But in this period the charge of sodomy was inconsistently applied and few executions under the law are recorded until the late 18th century.

In reality the economic structure of feudal society ruled out any real sexual autonomy for the vast majority of people. The household was at the centre of economic activity, producing the necessities of life through hard physical work on the land and small-scale domestic production. Survival outside of these structures was extremely difficult. Marriages among the poor were often arranged, and when one partner in a marriage died, the other would have to remarry. So familial and sexual relationships were tied very tightly into economic relationships and had little to do with emotional or sexual satisfaction. The economic ties were further tightened by the power of the local lord and the church.

However, in the growing urban centres across Europe new market relations were undermining the power of the old institutions of the landlord, church and family. Here a greater range of sexual choices seemed possible and a subculture emerged in which men chose freely to have sex with other men.

The development of capitalism accelerated these changes, opening up the way for sexuality to become an intensely contested arena. But as the rising capitalist class reached for new forms of sexual control and repression, they were to meet new forms of rebellion and resistance.

2: The rise of capitalism – a new oppression, a new resistance

The capitalist system emerged from a series of massive struggles which raised the prospect of an end to centuries of privilege and tyranny and of new rights based on "liberty, equality, fraternity", including sexual freedom.

In fact the rise of capitalism was to bring a new ruling class to power, the bourgeoisie, and with it new forms of exploitation and oppression – including sexual oppression. But in order to fully realise that power, they needed to break the stranglehold of the old feudal order. Fundamentally this meant freeing the economic forces and relationships that had begun to develop in the belly of the old society. This required challenging the institutions and prejudices on which feudalism rested: the divine right of the monarchy and aristocracy to rule along with the deference to hierarchy, superstition and tradition which came with it. Such struggles could not be waged successfully without rallying the mass of the population. So whether it was the landless poor and peasantry alongside the "middling sort" in the English Revolution, or the sansculottes in France, these revolts and revolutions drew people into political action on a huge scale.

In this context there developed new and radical ways of looking at the world, including the family, sexuality and relationships between men and women.

During the English Revolution in the mid-17th century a host of different religious and political groups flourished, some of which wanted a more complete transformation of society than simply the replacement of the king with a government of wealthy men. They brought with them new ideas about women and sexual morality which, however confused or limited, reflected a desire for more equal relationships and personal liberties in love.

The Levellers, for example, who saw the rights to one's own tools of production as a basic premise for economic freedom from the big exploiters, related these ideas to the notion of personal rights over one's own body. In the words of Richard Overton, "Everyone, as he is himselfe, so he hath a self-propriety, else could he not be himself." The Diggers, who wanted to abolish private property completely and replace it with communal ways of living, produced a series of pamphlets dealing with marriage and the family which talked of the "free liberty to marry whom they love" without regard to "birth nor portion",[26] while Lawrence Clarkson of the Ranters, who dreamt of a world free from the "rich and mighty", talked of a love free from the judgements of the mighty: "What act soever is done by thee in light and love, is light and lovely... No matter what Scripture, saints and churches say, if that within thee do not condemn thee, thou shalt not be condemned".[27]

The new revolutionary government of France decriminalised sex between men in 1791 and replaced it with a new code in which "true crimes" and not "those phoney offences created by superstition, feudalism, the tax system and despotism" were to be punished. Many countries across Europe followed suit even where sodomy had previously carried the death penalty. The American Revolution in 1766 against British colonial rule also decriminalised sodomy. The great bourgeois revolutions of the 17th and 18th centuries generated a mass following for ideas of equality and freedom from oppression which could easily be extended to the black slave, women and sexual freedoms.

The rights of man, the rights of woman

Tom Paine declared in his book *The Rights of Man* that, "Every age and generation must be as free to act for itself in all cases as the age and generations which preceded it." Mary Wollstonecraft insisted in her *A Vindication of the Rights of Woman* that the new freedoms also applied to women. She proclaimed against marriage, "for I don't want to be tied to this nasty world", and demanded women be free to pursue their "own whims where they lead, without having a husband and half a hundred children at hand". Both of these pamphlets enjoyed a wide circulation and helped to popularise the ideas associated with the Enlightenment, centrally that reason and knowledge could allow us to understand the world and shape a new society in opposition to the old authorities of religion, superstition and tradition. Thus many opposed the criminalisation of sexual acts between consenting adults even if, like Voltaire, one of the leading figures in the Enlightenment, they did not necessarily break with a personal disgust at a "vice destructive of the human race". Others who attacked the irrational victimisation of sodomy included the Italian philosopher Cesare Beccaria, who called for an end to laws of "utterly barbarous centuries", and English liberal thinker Jeremy Bentham, who wrote a series of private manuscripts against the oppression of same-sex activity.

The echo of revolution in everyday life

These ideas were informed by and helped to shape a popular consciousness. During his trial for sodomy in 1726 the young labourer William Brown declared in his defence, "I think there is no crime in making what use I please of my own body".[28] In France a tailor arrested by police in 1785 claimed "that he was not the only one, that he was harming nobody but himself, that he had given himself over to it very young, and that it was in his blood", while an 1817 pamphlet in Holland complained, "Everybody knows that these scoundrels among their equals openly speak of their gruesome lusts as something that is natural and proper to them".[29]

All of these examples carry the echo of an era of revolution, but what made their articulation possible was the way in which broader social and economic changes were shaking the old structures of social control.

As growing numbers of people were drawn into urban areas, the ties between personal life, the traditional family and old conventions began to loosen. At the same time those engaged in small-scale manufacturing or trading in the towns experienced home and work as two separate spheres. This opened up different possibilities for sexual experiences and relationships outside of the old patterns as is evidenced in the emergence of subcultures based around men having sex with each other in the urban centres of Western Europe from the late 17th century. In England this was centred on the molly houses: "'regular meeting places, pubs and back room clubs in which men drank and danced together, flirted with one another, held drag balls and imitated feminine mannerisms, and indulged in hugging, kissing, tickling each other as if they were a mixture of wanton males and females,' as a contemporary put it... The men involved were members of the working population of London: masters, journeymen and apprentices representing most of the city's manufacturing trade".[30]

Quite how widespread such activities were and what they meant in terms of "everyday life" is difficult to discern, since a lot of what we do know is drawn from surveillance, arrests and court cases of the time. An English verse of the 1770s, however, suggests that same-sex liaisons in the growing urban centres were not uncommon and were certainly widely known about:

> Observe this rule – ne'er pull your breeches off
> from health restoring slumbers strike to keep
> or ten to one you are buggered in your sleep.[31]

William Brown's defence in 1726 is nothing like the expression of a modern gay identity based around sexual preference, but it suggests the development among a layer of people of a belief that they had the right to engage in sexual activity free from interference.

The meaning of freedom – imposing a new order

This was not, however, how the British ruling class saw things. Throughout the 1700s sodomy remained punishable by death and continued to be referred to as "the abominable and detestable crime against nature". Although capital punishment was rarely used in the 1700s, the murder of a plasterer during a vicious pillory against him and his partner, a coachman, in 1780 was a warning of the kind of brutality that could be meted out and a precursor to a very bloody period from the late 18th century into the 19th century in which persecution of same sex acts was intensified.[32]

Why, at a time when many countries were relaxing their controls on sexual activity, was Britain stepping them up? The key to understanding this lies not in appreciating the peculiarities of the English, but in understanding the nature of the capitalist system.

The earliest revolution to establish a capitalist society took place in England, so that by the time of the French Revolution the English bourgeoisie had been in power for over a century. Their wealth came from the profits generated by a new and growing working class who, having been forced off the land, found they had no choice but to seek work in squalid factories and industrialised farms. The conditions were horrific – filth, misery and poverty reigned. In this situation the bourgeoisie feared that the radical struggles and ideas against privilege sweeping Europe might be taken up and turned against them. After all, the new freedoms they had promised to the poor and downtrodden on coming to power, such as free labour, had turned out to be a new form of servitude – wage labour. People with no access to land to produce a livelihood faced the "freedom" to starve or sell the only thing they had left at their disposal – their labour power.

> The bourgeoisie had not yet finished fighting its own battles to clear away the debris of feudalism in much of Europe. But it was already creating alongside itself a new exploited class capable of turning the revolutionary language of the French Revolution against the bourgeoisie itself.[33]

The fight over the role of the family in society was an important element in that larger struggle by the bourgeoisie to crush this "revolutionary language" in order to assert its control over the working class.

Not only were the working class beginning to develop new forms of organisation to resist their exploitation in the corresponding committees and trade unions, but they were doing so at a time when an older form of organisation, the family, was breaking up on a dramatic scale. Having been ripped away from working arrangements that had centred on the family, people found themselves thrown into huge urban areas, "each standing alone in the labour market".[34] As the economic relationships previously associated with the family were stripped away, established hierarchies also broke down. Capitalists seeking to cheapen their costs turned to the labour of women and children and technological innovations were used to displace men and women from their traditional areas of work:

> In many cases the family is not wholly dissolved by the
> employment of the wife, but turned upside down. The wife
> supports the family; the husband sits at home, tends the chil-
> dren, sweeps the room and cooks.[35]

The disintegration of a tried and tested institution, and
the relationships of authority that went with it, began to
worry sections of the bourgeoisie who feared the ways it
could feed into a wider unrest and threaten their ability to
maintain social control. The efficient organisation of capitalist industry required a deference to hierarchy and discipline
which the family had traditionally instilled and it was
thought better that workers be tied into their individual families by a sense of responsibility and the need to be
self-sufficient, than be drawn towards the collective organisations of class warfare.

Some capitalists also began to fear the ways the general
immiseration of the working class and the collapse of family
support were having a dramatic effect on the health and
mortality of workers. An inquiry in Liverpool showed the
average life expectancy of machine operatives to be "but 15
years". In Manchester it was reported that "57 percent of
the children of the working class perish before the fifth year".
Investigations in Wolverhampton discovered the appallingly
low level of education: "A boy, 17 years old, did not know
how many two and two made, nor how many farthings there
were in twopence, even when the money was placed in his
hand".[36]

For a section of the bourgeoisie who wanted a healthy,
disciplined, educated workforce that could be easily replen-
ished, this was a major worry. But it also represented a threat
to the legitimacy of an institution that continued to be central
to the bourgeoisie as a means to concentrate their wealth and

protect their property.

While material conditions were causing workers' families to break apart, the bourgeoisie was taking steps to strengthen the institution legally and ideologically to serve its needs as a class. The 1753 Marriage Act turned marriage from a verbal agreement into a legal contract and removed a woman's rights to property, income and children. This was aimed at reinforcing the family as a means of protecting the wealth of the bourgeoisie. As one contemporary put it, "consider what importance to society the chastity of women is. Upon that all the property in the world depends. We hang a thief for stealing a sheep; but the unchastity of a woman transfers sheep and farm and all from the right owner".[37] The woman had become property of her husband.

But as a class which had come to power claiming to challenge the inherited dynasties of the aristocracy, the bourgeoisie needed a new set of ideas around which to build the family. The legal contract was to be sealed on the basis of a relationship formed through mutual choice and romantic love. By the 19th century its centre, the home, was to be a private haven in which the bourgeoisie could enjoy their wealth and protect their women, children and property. This emphasis on individual choice in relationships and the ideology of domesticity, which stressed the home as a place of stability, virtue and self-cultivation, provided important values for a bourgeoisie seeking to shape society in its image and differentiate itself from the decadent aristocracy and immoral lower orders.

The public discussion of relationships recognised that people were entitled to a sexual life but this was to be expressed within marriage and in terms which allowed the head of the family (the man) to set the agenda. As a popular 1850s book about sexuality explained:

> I should say that the majority of women (happily for society) are not very much troubled with sexual feeling of any kind...

THE RED IN THE RAINBOW

Many of the best mothers, wives and managers of households know little or are careless about sexual indulgences. Love of home, of children and domestic duties are the only passion they feel.[38]

This need to deny women's sexuality independent of men is certainly a major reason why sex between women did not become a target for the ruling class in the way it did for men. But despite the absence of direct attacks or laws against lesbianism, the family structure, ideology and prejudice played a powerful role in policing women's sexuality. The weaker economic position of women and their marginality to public life compared to men, combined with the invisibility accorded to female sexuality, made it very difficult for women to develop the kind of gay subculture developed by men.

But the invisibility effect was contradictory. It meant, for example, that some women were able to enjoy lasting, physically intimate relationships because they were assumed to be non-sexual. Such "romantic friendships", as they have since become known, were clearly sexual in some cases, but there are also many instances of women who enjoyed deep relationships, or settled down and lived together where we simply don't know. The Ladies of Llangollen, for example, were two upper class Irish women who eloped in 1778 to set up home in Wales where they lived for the rest of their lives. They were regarded as reputable, enjoyed many respectable visitors and even got a pension from the king, though one guest confided that she could not "help thinking that surely it was not platonic, heaven forgive me I look within myself and doubt."

During this period there were also working class women who "passed" as men, doing men's work and having sexual relationships with other women, including getting married to them. Their incentives for doing so could include gaining access to higher wages as well as seeking greater personal and sexual freedom, but again such relations between women survived because they were effectively unseen, so we cannot know the extent of them.

In 1921, when parliament tried to extend laws against male homosexuality to women, it was rejected by the House of Lords. As Lord Desart the Director of Public Prosecution put it:

> You are going to tell the whole world that there is such an offence, to bring it to the notice of women who have never heard of it, never thought of it, never dreamt of it. I think that would be a very great mischief.

The disintegration of the family and the breakdown of the old sexual order appeared to present multiple risks to the bourgeoisie, both in terms of its economic system and the values on which it rested. It became "a striking metaphor" for the threat of social unrest and even revolution.

During the wars with France from 1793 to 1815, for example, the British ruling class attempted to conjure up old fears of disaster and evil by linking the French Revolution to sodomy and sexual licence and the threat it presented of a "revolution in ethical, moral and religious spheres".

Bourgeois society was also obsessed with the sexual depravity of the "lower orders". Factory commissions complained about the "bestial and filthy desires" of male workers and the "unchastity" of factory girls working half naked in sweltering conditions. Investigations into the overcrowded slums were gripped by the risks they carried of "sexual promiscuity and even sexual perversion". There were recurring themes of working men with predatory drives, increasing levels of teenage sexuality and prostitution, and the dire effect of factory work on women which, according to a Dr Barnardo's report, was encouraging a "spirit of precocious independence which weakens family ties and is highly unfavourable to the growth of domestic virtues".[39]

The bourgeoisie was certainly not united in how to respond to these problems, but in grappling to take control a number of measures were introduced that bolstered the family and attacked sexual activities and practices that might threaten it.

A series of Factory Acts in 1833, 1842 and 1844 restricting the age, hours and type of place children and women could work were introduced under the pressure of mass agitation by workers against horrendous conditions. These were bitterly opposed by many employers who wanted to be free to exploit without restrictions, but other sections of the ruling class saw the long-term benefits of reforms which could help ensure a more healthy workforce and encourage family values. For workers these reforms appeared to offer the best means of achieving some improvements in their living standards, but they also had the effect of undermining women's independence and encouraging the idea that her place was not in the workplace but in the home.

The acts were accompanied by the punitive Poor Law of 1834. This was aimed at forcing workers to accept poverty wages by refusing "outdoor relief" in the form of food, money or clothes to the "able-bodied" and unmarried women with children. People who could not support themselves were forced to work in the prison-like poorhouse; a very public punishment which acted as a constant moral warning of the terrible fate that would become those who shied away from their family responsibilities.

> To prevent the superfluous from multiplying and demoralised parents from influencing their children, families are broken up; the husband is placed in one wing, the wife in another, the children in a third, and they are permitted to see one another only at stated times after long intervals, and then only when they have, in the opinion of the officials, behaved well.[40]

Alongside the failed family and undeserving poor, the

sodomite also proved a convenient scapegoat for the ruling class. As Norah Carlin argues:

> better they [workers] should mob sodomites than riot for reforms or against corrupt government. The men who went to the gallows and the pillory were indeed a symbolic sacrifice, but the dangers they symbolised were new ones. The old triad of heresy, witchcraft and sodomy had been replaced by the new one of sodomy, mutiny and anarchy.[41]

Thus the first rise in the number of executions for sodomy occurred in 1797 during the naval mutinies. Between 1806 and 1836 executions for sodomy increased to an average of around two a year, at a time when the death penalty for many other sentences was being drastically reduced. In 1806, for example, more people were executed for sodomy than murder and in 1810 four out of five people convicted for sodomy were hanged.[42] This contrasts with the period of 1730 to 1750, when the Old Bailey heard only one case a year connected to sodomy, and with the years 1749 to 1790, when only two men were executed for sodomy.[43]

A series of laws in the 1820s introduced new offences, to include "attempts at, solicitation of, persuasion to, and even promises of" sodomy.[44] This increased the numbers of men who were convicted of attempted sodomy, rather than sodomy itself, typically carrying a sentence of two years. This was a stepping stone towards the much broader law of 1885 which targeted all sexual acts between men.

The increased level of surveillance of sexual activities was part of a wider attempt at controlling the new urban working class. Previously the law had been left to local discretion and occasional spectacular displays of brutality, such as the pillory and public executions. When necessary the army could always be brought in. But these methods were less effective and even counterproductive against a working class which was beginning to organise strikes, mass demonstrations, uprisings and civil disobedience. So alongside the establishment of the Metropolitan Police in 1829 – or the "blue butchers" as they became known by working class activists – the ruling class developed a set of laws to systematically police forms of behaviour. The Vagrancy Acts of the 1800s, for example, which prohibited "a disorderly way of living", could be used against the unemployed, the dissident, the prostitute or the sodomite. These laws went hand in hand with a set of moral panics against so-called immoral sexual practices among the "lower orders" such as prostitution, "hyper breeding", illegitimacy and incest.

There was resistance to these new forms of social control. Mass demonstrations took place against the setting up of local police forces and in 1833 a verdict of "justifiable homicide" returned on the killing of a policeman reflected the widespread hostility towards them.[45] Opposition to the police also shaped people's responses to the policing of sodomy: the surveillance and entrapment of men engaged in same-sex acts was widely distrusted and there was a cynicism at the double standard surrounding the prosecution of working class men and women for sexual activities which the privileged classes got away with.[46] The Poor Law also sparked bitter opposition. Protests and attacks on workhouses meant that they couldn't be introduced for over a decade in some areas.

Chartism, new utopias and free love

This resistance was part of a rising level of working class struggle from 1815 that culminated in the first mass working class movement in history, Chartism. The significance of Chartism went way beyond its formal demands for radical democratic reform based on universal suffrage. It was the first working class organisation in the world that sought to go beyond individual acts of revolt by creating a "permanent organisation with its own democratic structures".[47] Its activities between 1838 and 1850 spanned the first general strike and a mass confrontation with parliament and the state.

These struggles generated a belief among many working class people that radical change, even revolution, was possible, and shaped a context in which those who talked about fighting for a future based on genuine freedom for all, including freedom in love and equality between the sexes, could gain a hearing.

Radicals associated with the early socialist movement at the turn of the 19th century, such as Claude Henri de Saint-Simon, Charles Fourier and Robert Owen, enjoyed a growing following. Later described by Engels as the utopian socialists, they shared a common project of campaigning for a new world in which sexual liberation and women's emancipation would be realised.

Their ideas were shaped by the Enlightenment optimism about the potential of science and industry to shape a new world and the promise of new freedom. They regarded the restrictions on women and love as one of the most potent symbols of the betrayal of those hopes by the bourgeoisie. Fourier, for example, argued in his book *Theories of Four Movements* that "the measure of general emancipation" in society must be judged by "the degree of emancipation of women".

The utopian socialists argued that women were "reduced to a state of slavery" within marriage, trivialised in the home, "the eternal prison house of the wife", denied freedom in love, and treated like "a passive machine for producing children". In place of this situation they advocated alternative ways of living. Saint-Simon called for "free love" and "moral unions". Owen and followers of Fourier set up communities that replaced competition with mutual cooperation, and offered collective living arrangements where "domestic drudgery" and child rearing were shared. The status of illegitimacy was also abolished.

Utopian socialism expressed the "first instinctive yearnings" of the oppressed and exploited "for a general reconstruction of society", but it had developed during a period of political reaction when the working class had barely emerged as a political force. As a result the early socialists tended to view workers as victims rather than the potential creators of a new society, and to regard themselves as grand reformers who would win society round by good arguments and through the example of building model communities. But this top-down, elitist approach to changing the world undermined some of the emancipatory elements in utopian socialist thought. The same rational organisation of society which could liberate women from the drudgery of housework could also be used to make the workers more productive for capitalism. And if the rich only needed to be convinced of the benefits of socialism then appealing to them should be a priority since they had the wealth and resources to make it happen.

Robert Owen, who used his position as a mill owner to oversee an experiment in the new life at New Lanark mill in the early 1800s, spent a large part of his early political life trying to persuade other wealthy philanthropists to fund similar communities on the basis that it would improve the productivity of their workers. The mill was one of the largest factories in the world and did offer more humane conditions for the workers there. However, many later experiments ended in failure and achieved little reach inside the working class. As Owen himself acknowledged, New Lanark achieved small practical improvements for the workers involved but failed to match up to the vision of a new emancipated society: "the people remained slaves at my mercy."

So while the utopian socialists dared to imagine another world was possible, they were unable to pinpoint how this fundamental transformation of society would be achieved.

They appealed to all classes, not recognising that the capitalist class had every material interest in opposing their project for a new world, and put too much store in the power of rational argument disconnected from a working class struggle that could give those arguments some power.

The growing resistance to the injustices of capitalism in the 1830s and 40s, however, began to point the way to the kind of struggles that might be able to achieve such "utopias", and created a bigger audience among those waging these struggles for new ideas about women and sexuality: "Debates on the abolition of marriage and illegitimacy, proposals for the replacement of family life by collective housekeeping, and arguments about women's right to work and to be trade union members all flourished among Owenite workers".[48]

Socialists also took part in relationships described as "free unions" snubbing the need for formal recognition of their relationships from the church or state and were among the early agitators to promote contraception and support for freedom to control one's own sexuality. The popularity among workers of Romantic poets such as Shelley, whose *Queen Mab* declared "love withers under constraint", and Lord Byron, who celebrated homosexual love, worried the ruling class. The meshing together of utopian socialist ideas about how society could be organised differently, with those of the Romantic poets who railed against the constraints of the old world, shaped a radical sexual politics among some involved in the workers' movement.

These ideas were by no means uncontroversial or dominant. Another response among workers to the horrors of the factories and slums was to seek refuge in the family. As one woman Chartist put it:

> We have seen that because the husband's earnings could not support his family, the wife has been compelled to leave her home neglected and, with her infant children, work at a soul and body

degrading toil... For years we have struggled to maintain our homes in comfort such as our hearts told us should greet our husbands after their fatiguing labours. Year after year has passed away, and even now our wishes have no prospect of being realised, our husbands are overwrought, our houses half-furnished, our families ill-fed and our children uneducated.[49]

However, at a time when the bourgeoisie was seeking to extinguish the dreams and hopes inspired by the revolutionary struggles that had bought it to power, the working class was emerging as a force that could carry those dreams forward. At a time when the bourgeoisie was turning its back on any notion of freedom in love, sections of the working class movement were beginning to link their fight for freedom to the fight for the rights of women and the freedom to love.

Realising the dream of a new world

The great struggles of Chartism in England were part of a growing revolt which culminated in the 1848 revolutions across Europe, shaking the old governments and winning democratic reforms. These struggles also shaped the birth of Marxism and a scientific socialism that was able to fuse the dreams of the utopian socialists with a recognition that the working class had the power to achieve them. As Marx declared in the founding statement of the First International Workingmen's Association, "The emancipation of the working class must be conquered by the working classes themselves."

The belief in human liberation at the heart of early socialism remained central to Marxism, but was now connected to a theory of the working class as the group with the interest and economic power to achieve it. Workers could be the "gravediggers of capitalism" because the capitalist system rested on the exploitation of their collective labour.

The minority class of the bourgeoisie had shaped the

family by law and ideology into an instrument that defended and reproduced an unequal society in which workers were exploited, women oppressed and any variation in sexuality persecuted. Marx argued that it was in the interests of the working class majority in society to create "a new economical foundation for a higher family form and relations between the sexes" free from exploitation and oppression. Hence the working class was the "universal class" with the interest and the power to create a new socialist society that would set everybody free.

This would not be achieved by imposing blueprints for a better world from above, or by seeking small reforms within existing society, but required a revolutionary struggle, "not only", Marx said, "because the ruling class cannot be overthrown in any other way, but also because the class overthrowing it can only in a revolution succeed in ridding itself of all the muck of ages and become fitted to found society anew".[50] This was why Engels argued that "with every great revolution free love comes to the fore". Revolution is about challenging all of the prejudices and oppressions on which class society rests, and it is the only means by which we can leap from "the realm of necessity" to the "realm of freedom".

The utopian socialists, along with Marx and Engels, were operating at a time when modern sexual identities and lifestyles based around sexual preference had yet to develop, and they did not deal explicitly with same-sex relationships, but argued in general terms against women's oppression and restrictions on sexual love. Nevertheless we can see that socialists took oppression seriously and attempted to integrate the fight for sexual freedom and women's liberation into the fight for a new world. This provided an important framework for a later generation of socialists faced with more systematic attacks by the ruling class on what came to be categorised as sexual minorities.

Reaction

The power of these ideas lay in the workers' struggle in England and revolts across Europe, but as they were defeated a period of experimentation in the working class was replaced by a period of reaction. In England those who looked to the private family as the best means of defending their conditions became much more dominant.

The family was seen as a solution from above and below. The ruling class regarded it as a cheaper method of reproducing a new generation of workers than mass childcare and the improvement of working and living conditions. Many workers considered it a more realistic answer to their problems in a period where more fundamental change seemed impossible.

The idea of the family wage, which meant the male breadwinner would earn enough to keep his wife and children at home, became popular. It was seen as a means of protecting women and children from hellish working conditions, of stopping the bosses using them to undercut wages, and of providing some kind of decent home life. But ideologically it was a backward step that involved conceding to reactionary ideas about women's place being in the home. It also undercut the ability of workers to fight for a general raising of wages and conditions for all. The family did little to cushion the effects of poverty and exploitation of workers, but it became a potent aspiration for workers seeking shelter from the harsh conditions of life.

It was reinforced by the entrenchment of forms of organisation inside the working class which became much more narrowly focused on protecting the interests of sections of the working class within the status quo – shifting away from the transformative politics of the mass movements and struggles that had gone before. The craft unions which grew in the 1850s and 1860s, for example, based their power on the ability of skilled workers to negotiate bread and butter improvements in their trade to the exclusion of unskilled and women workers who had played such a major role in previous struggles.

In the same period there developed a much stronger consensus among the ruling class about the importance of the family in ensuring the profitability of British capitalism. The development of more sophisticated production techniques required a higher level of skill and education among workers who as a result became less dispensable. In this situation it just didn't do to have a quarter of children in Manchester dying before their first birthday – a statistic from the 1860s.

The ruling class employed a combination of bribes, reforms and repressive measures to enforce a very narrow form of the family. Alongside the promotion of the family wage, a series of factory and education acts were introduced which limited the industries and hours women could work and extended state education for children to age 13. Understandably these measures were welcomed by many workers as progress, but they were imposed on terms which enabled the bourgeoisie to place the main burden of reproducing, bringing up and caring for workers and their children onto working class families, and specifically women.

The promotion of the bourgeois family across the whole of society had the effect of entrenching it as not only the most desirable, but the *only* way to live. It involved the creation of a series of new categories which sought to naturalise the roles on which it depended – the housewife, the mother and childhood. It also stigmatised those whose lifestyles or behaviour were seen to challenge the function of the family and gender roles that went with it.

The restriction of sexuality was especially important because of the way in which the growing urban areas were increasing opportunities for people to more openly express variations in sexuality. In the drive to clamp down on these activities a much more systematic attack on "deviant sexualities" was developed in which two major groups were targeted – prostitutes and men having sex with men.

There had been a growing worry about the spread of venereal disease, especially in the army where one in three cases of illness were said to be caused by it. A series of contagious diseases acts in the 1860s introduced measures which allowed the forcible internal examination and up to nine months' internment of women suspected of suffering from venereal disease. The same standards were not applied to men. This gave the state extraordinary powers to police working class communities:

> Under the acts extramarital sex became a question of state policy... Special controls were placed on the female body in that prostitutes, not their male clients, were identified as the primary source of disease and pollution. This medical and police supervision in turn created an outcast class of sexually deviant women, forcing prostitutes to acknowledge their status as "public" women and destroying their private association with the general community of the labouring poor.[51]

This tendency to criminalise the prostitute rather than the activity of prostitution was later in the 19th century to be used to even more devastating effect in the categorisation and oppression of "the homosexual". This was a key transition in the treatment of same-sex desire and activity from regarding it as a "temporary aberration", which in theory anyone could engage in, to an intrinsic characteristic of a type of person.

The love that dare not speak its name

Although the last execution for sodomy was in 1836 and the death penalty for the crime was abolished in 1861, the state continued to persecute sexual activity between men, even extending the terms on which they could be charged. Legislation against prostitutes became the means of ratcheting up the attacks against homosexuals.

An 1885 act centred on further controls over prostitution – raising the age of consent for girls, and making it easier to close down brothels – but was amended to include all acts of "gross indecency between men" in public *and private* punishable by up to two years' hard labour. Although this amendment was introduced almost by accident by the maverick MP Henry Labouchere, it proved to be a key staging post in the persecution of homosexuals because of the wider climate of moral panic being whipped up against supposed threats to the respectable family. That year alone had seen a quarter of a million people march against women falling victim to the "white slave trade" – the sexual trafficking of British women abroad, the extent of which was greatly exaggerated in the press. An 1898 law against prostitutes importuning was almost exclusively used against importuning by males, who also suffered much heavier sentences.

This was a time of rising anxiety among those in power about an economic depression, conflict in Ireland and Africa, and the sheer speed at which urban areas were growing. These anxieties gave an edge to the rhetoric and the laws about both prostitutes and homosexuals, who became convenient symbols of what was threatening the "purity of the family…the surest strength of a nation".[52]

Defence of family and nation was also invoked against the supposed sexual threat posed by Africa, Asia and the Middle East which Britain, along with other European countries, was busily colonising. Africans were demonised as sexually permissive and corrupt, and sodomy laws were introduced in the colonies to control them. Just as the "homosexual" proved to be a useful enemy within for the British ruling class, so the new category of "catamite" or "habitual sodomite" was developed to serve a similar pur-

　　　　　　　　　　　　THE RED IN THE RAINBOW

pose in Africa and other colonised areas. Racism, colonial oppression and homophobia marched hand in hand.

A series of trials in the 1880s and 1890s in Britain gave a very public profile to the homosexual. The most significant of these was the trial of Oscar Wilde, who had failed to have the Marquess of Queensberry convicted of libel when he alleged that Wilde was "posing as a sodomite". As a consequence Wilde was charged and found guilty under the 1885 Act with gross indecency and sentenced to two years' hard labour, the judge declaring Wilde's crime "worse than murder". His life was destroyed and a very public line was drawn against this "deviant" behaviour. It is a great irony that Wilde, a man married with two children, should become the most powerful symbol of the "impassable border" between deviant and non-deviant sexuality. The *Evening News* declared during the trial, "We venture to hope that the conviction of Wilde for these abominable vices, which were the natural outcome of this diseased intellectual condition, will be a salutary warning to the unhealthy boys who posed as sharers of his culture".[53] It was not a great leap from this to Lord Summer in 1918 referring to homosexuals as carrying "the hallmark of a specialised and extraordinary class as much as if they had carried on their bodies some physical peculiarities".[54]

The outcast of one age, the hero of another

But the witch-hunt against Wilde had a contradictory effect. During his trial Wilde made a passionate speech in defence of "the love that dare not speak its name" declaring, "It is beautiful, it is fine, it is the noblest form of affection…that it should be so the world does not understand." For many this expression of a love they had felt or experienced in silence was the beginning of a moment of self-definition. One of the early sexual reformers in Britain, Havelock Ellis, commented that the trial seemed "to have generally contributed to give definiteness and self-consciousness to the manifestations of homosexuality and to have aroused inverts to take a definite stand".[55]

For many this stand was tentative, individualised and often imbued with an acceptance that homosexuals carried a mark of inferiority. But there were others who were beginning to develop more political responses and seeking collective forms of resistance. This was not only a time when the powerful were stirring up moral panics about sexual deviants. It was also a time of struggle against the powerful. There was the long-running opposition to British rule in Ireland, a revival in socialist ideas and a shaking up of old union conservatism by the explosion of New Unionism in 1889-91 – a wave of strikes and resistance involving hundreds of thousands of unskilled and women workers.

These events helped to shape the responses of a number of homosexual rights pioneers in Britain including Edward Carpenter, John Addington Symonds and Havelock Ellis. They were all involved in the socialist and working class movement which connected them with the early utopian tradition and some of the new ideas around women's and homosexual emancipation developing in the international socialist movement, in such texts as Engels's *The Origin of the Family, Private Property and the State* and August Bebel's *Women and Socialism*.

Edward Carpenter, for example, took up many of the early socialist themes of free love, women's emancipation, opposition to bourgeois conventions in marriage and the link between the alienation of labour and sexual relationships. He also took the "propaganda of the deed" very seriously and spent the latter part of his life living openly with his male lover in a semi-commune in Sheffield, cycling around working class areas giving out pamphlets on free love and spreading the word. These socialist traditions had been kept alive among the sons and daughters of Chartists and groups of workers who continued to identify with and practice a form of Owenism. But they were being developed and expressed by Carpenter within the framework of a newly emerging homosexual identity. One of his major inspirations was the late romantic gay poet Walt Whitman, who celebrated "the love of comrades". He was also influenced by the early campaigners for the rights of homosexual love across the continent.

As early as the 1860s the German campaigning lawyer Karl-Heinrich Ulrichs had written a series of pamphlets called *Researches into the Riddle of Love between Men* in which he defended Uranian love (derived from Plato's heavenly love in *Symposium*). He developed a number of terms for the homosexual man (*Urning*), homosexual woman (*Urningin*) and bisexual (*Uranodioning* or *Uranodioningin*). In the same decade human rights activist and journalist Karl-Maria Benkert had defended the rights of the "homosexual" in an open letter to the German minister of justice against new laws being introduced in Germany. Both rested their defence on the notion that homosexuality was inborn and therefore should be unpunishable. By the 1880s these ideas were widespread among the early pioneers of homosexual rights, many of whom were connected to the medical profession.

Carpenter took these ideas up and gave a special role to the homosexual in the creation of the "new life". It is possible, he argued:

> that the Uranian spirit may lead to something like a general enthusiasm of humanity, and that the Uranian people may be destined to form the advance guard of that great movement which will one day transform common life by substituting the land of personal affection and compassion for the monetary, legal and other external ties which now control and confine society.[56]

The notion that homosexuals, or Uranians, as Carpenter called them, were somehow biologically distinct from heterosexuals is something that most LGBT activists today would rightly oppose. But at the time the positive assertion of a homosexual identity, however distorted, was a very important rejection of the hysteria being whipped up against sex between men. Early medical theories around sexuality had been developed for use in criminal hearings in order to "give evidence" against those accused of committing sodomy, and then "homosexuality". In that context it was important that others in the medical profession emerged with the motive of defending people against such criminalisation, even if they still accepted what we would now consider very dubious ideas about the biological basis for homosexuality.

Just as important was the attempt to link this struggle for the right of people to love without persecution to the working class struggle against capitalism. Carpenter would regularly speak to working class audiences numbering hundreds and sometimes thousands. The importance of this was brought home in the year following the trial of Oscar Wilde when the Manchester Labour Press printed and sold thousands of copies of Carpenter's *Love's Coming of Age* following the decision by his publisher to drop it for fear of scandal or legal action.

Despite this act of solidarity, Carpenter's view of the relationship between the dream of a new utopia based on "the love of comrades" and the working class movement remained abstract. His adage "The outcast of one age is the hero of another" reflected a view that it was the dispossessed and outcast, rather than organised workers, who were carriers of a new society. This gap between revolutionary aspirations and day-to-day agitation inside the working class was a general weakness in the British left, whose traditions had been shaped by a long period of defeat inside the working class over the preceding decades.

The renewed agitation of the 1880s and militant burst of new unionism had heralded a new chapter in working class resistance. It also helped to shape the beginnings of a new sexual politics. But the decline of the movement meant that Carpenter, Ellis and Symonds, while representing an important transition towards the development of a new gay consciousness, had no mass working class struggle to connect those ideas to.

It was in Germany, home to the largest working class party in the world, that the relationship between a new homosexual identity and the working class movement was to be forged and the first mass homosexual rights organisation born

Logo from the German edition (1923) of Grigorii Batkis's
The Sexual Revolution in Russia

3: The two souls of sexual liberation – reform and revolution in Germany and Russia

By the turn of the 20th century Germany was at the heart of the international socialist movement and home to the Scientific Humanitarian Committee (SHC) – the first homosexual rights organisation in the world. The SHC had been launched in 1897 with the declared aim of overturning Germany's anti-homosexual law, Paragraph 175. Its most important founding member, Magnus Hirschfeld, was also a member of the German Social Democratic Party (SPD), the biggest working class organisation in the world, with a million members and massive influence not only over the politics, but also the social and cultural lives of the working class.

The SPD and SHC both emerged in the context of rapid industrialisation in Germany, which had become the world's second biggest economy by 1900. Some cities had doubled in size within a matter of decades. These became home to a working class which joined the SPD in their thousands, and a gay subculture that flourished in the new urban centres. In both the Ruhr and Berlin, for example, gay areas developed alongside the huge industrial complexes based around electrical engineering, steel and iron.

The speed of development meant that the old rubbed very starkly against the new. Many workers still lived and worked in small towns and villages but others were fast being drawn into big cities and mass production. The removal of feudal walls that had once surrounded different trade centres opened up new public areas, such as the vast urban parks, which allowed opportunities for sexual encounters outside of the old constraints.[57]

But all of these developments took place under the regime of the Prussian monarchy. Unlike in France, the German bourgeoisie had failed to lead a successful revolution against the old order. They settled instead for a compromise with the landowning aristocracy, who continued to hold the political reins while adapting to the interests of industry and the capitalist class. The compromise was reflected in the political institutions that dominated society. Parliament was elected by universal male suffrage, but had very little power. The government was appointed by the Emperor. The SPD was illegal until 1890, and continued to suffer semi-legal status from then on.

Yet at the same time, the rapid expansion of German capitalism enabled the ruling class to make concessions to the working class as a means of containing unrest. Wages rose, small welfare benefits were introduced and some union organisation established. The SPD, forced by its semi-legal position to seek every opportunity to build its influence, was able to sink deep roots into every area of working class life. By 1900 it was producing up to 90 daily newspapers, running a huge range of societies from sports clubs to stamp collecting groups, and employing hundreds of full-time workers.

The contradictory situation facing the workers' movement was in some ways mirrored by that facing the newly emerging gay subculture. Prior to the unification of Germany in 1871, sex between men had been legal in a number of kingdoms. The new German state introduced a blanket ban on homosexuality, at the same time as accelerating the expansion of new urban areas in which a gay subculture could develop. One result of this was the explosion of publications on homosexuality, with 320 published in 1896 alone. By 1914 in Berlin around 40 gay bars existed and police estimate there were between 1,000 and 2,000 male prostitutes.[58]

The size of the SPD, and its influence not only in the workplace but across society, meant it could be seen as a very

THE RED IN THE RAINBOW

powerful organisation by someone like Hirschfeld seeking to win political reform for homosexuals. The socialist movement also had a strong tradition of support for the oppressed.

Decades before, in the 1860s, when anti-sodomy laws were being introduced in Germany, socialists had defended the homosexual JB von Schweitzer during his trial for public indecency. They later elected him as the leader of the Universal Working Men's Association, during which time he was voted in as an MP in the Reichstag.

The SPD had also defended Oscar Wilde during his trial in 1895, using the pages of its mass circulation newspaper to challenge this witch-hunt. The occasion was used by leading member Eduard Bernstein to polemicise in favour of a socialist politics which openly discussed homosexuality and took sexual politics seriously:

> Although the subject of sex life might seem a low priority for the economic and political struggle of the Social Democracy this nevertheless does not mean it is not obligatory to find a standard also for judging this side of social life… Today the party is strong enough to exert influence on the character of statutory law, and through its speakers and press it enjoys an influence upon public opinion… As a result it must take a certain responsibility for what happens these days.[59]

This was followed by an "investigation" into sexuality by Bernstein in a series of articles which sought to show how moral attitudes were not a natural but "historical phenomena":

> Previously the Romans, the Greeks, the Egyptians and various Asiatic peoples cultivated homosexual gratification. Same-sex intercourse is so old and so widespread there is no state of human culture we can say with certainty was free from this phenomenon.

The attempt to look at how human sexuality is shaped by wider economic and social relationships in society was of major importance at a time when crude, essentialist categories were being imposed on human sexuality – and the dominant ideas even among sexual reformers tended to mirror this view. It represented an important attempt to apply the socialist theory of oppression and liberation to a newly emerging oppressed group.

The strength of the SPD and positions it took in support of homosexual rights were key to shaping the launch of the first homosexual rights organisation in the world.

In some ways the SHC seemed quite removed from a mass working class organisation. Hirschfeld was a campaigning doctor, and launched the organisation alongside a publisher and civil servant. Its goal to achieve "justice" for homosexuals "through science" reflected the dominant belief among progressive reformers and scientists that proving that homosexuality was inborn, and therefore neither a sin nor a crime, offered the best protection against criminalisation and victimisation.

This approach was understandable given the huge power vested in science at the time. Science was seen by many as the engine of the new world – particularly in Germany, where it was harnessed by a new state seeking to build its economic power and status. A number of advancements in embryology, the study of hormones and the rise of psychiatry also fed optimism in the ability of science to help understand sexuality and win homosexual rights.

However, the invention of new biological categories for lesbians and gays involved making concessions to some of the worst reactionary ideas about sexuality and gender. Hirschfeld, for example, dedicated a huge amount of research to developing pseudo-scientific theories about the "third sex" which argued homosexuals (women and men) combined elements of the male and female sex. Yet this notion that lesbians are more masculine and homosexual men more feminine concedes to the popular prejudices and gender stereotypes that underpin LGBT oppression. Although the SHC broke new ground in being the first political organisation dedicated to homosexual rights, it failed to challenge a medical paradigm that continued to be central in shaping lesbian and gay oppression at least until the 1960s, when a new movement began to reject such ideas.

The SHC's reformist approach assumed that rational argument would be enough to win the government to a change of heart. Their strategy focused on a petition which would garner names of "the opinion makers...prominent scientists, lawyers, educators, writers, highly placed civil servants, church functionaries".[60] This stress on "respectable" politics fitted with the aspirations of a layer of middle class homosexual men who, because of their economic and social position in society, were most able to articulate the newly emerging homosexual identity.[61]

Nevertheless, the SHC's organised attempt to mobilise science and medicine in support of homosexual rights represented a major step forward at the turn of the 20th century. There was also something quite new and exciting about its stated aim of "interesting the homosexual himself in the struggle for his rights". This notion was informed both by the emerging sense of a collective homosexual identity made possible in the urban areas, and the political tradition of the SPD which shaped a political environment in which a struggle by a persecuted minority could be conceived.

From the start the SPD stood alone among the parties in its support for the SHC.

Their members made up many of the initial signatories to the petition, and in 1898 August Bebel took it into the German parliament. Here he made the first ever recorded speech in favour of gay rights, shocking the establishment with claims about a homosexuality which "reaches so deeply into all social circles". In future parliamentary debates the SPD supported the petition in the face of fierce opposition from all the other parties.

This support was crucial in helping the SHC make homosexuality a major political issue of the day. By 1914 around 100,000 books and pamphlets had been produced on the subject, the most famous of which, *What the People should know about the Third Sex*, had gone into 19 editions by 1907. In the same year a debate on Paragraph 175 attracted 2,000 people. Hirschfeld's 1903 study of sexuality involved thousands of factory workers and students responding to questionnaires about their sexual activity and led to what were then considered astonishing conclusions: that at least 2.2 percent of the population, over one million Germans, were bisexual or gay!

Energy was also put into mobilising the "gay vote", with candidates confronted about their position on Paragraph 175 and appeals put out as follows: "Reichstag election! 3rd sex! Consider this! In the Reichstag on May 31, 1905, members of the Centre, the Conservatives and the economic Alliance spoke against you; but for you the orators of the Left! Agitate and vote accordingly!"[62] By 1910 over 5,000 self-professed homosexuals had contacted the SHC, with 1,000 joining, such that it could legitimately claim:

The period of passing the matter over in silence and disregarding it is past for good. We now find ourselves in the midst of a period of discussion. The homosexual question has become a genuine question, one which has given rise to lively debate, and which will continue to be discussed until it has been resolved in a satisfactory way.[63]

Despite the success in winning a section of public support, Hirschfeld and the SHC failed to bring together the campaign for homosexual rights with the mass membership of the largest working class party in the world in a systematic way. Instead their focus remained firmly on winning support among sections of the establishment for legal reform. This shaped a political conservatism which the SPD pointed out involved "a deep bow to the controlling Centre Party and to bigotry in general".[64]

But political conservatism in the SPD was not confined to Hirschfeld, and sexual politics proved to be a continual source of division and controversy inside the party. The party was divided over support for the repeal of Paragraph 175. Its newspaper *Die Zukunft* (the Future) played a very bad role during the Moltke-Harden-Eulenburg affair, a scandal in 1907-9, when in a series of editorials it attacked close advisers to the Kaiser and senior army officers on the basis of "secret immorality and unnatural vices". A series of trials and counter-libel trials regarding homosexual behaviour ensued. Although motivated by a desire to weaken a reactionary and undemocratic regime, *Die Zukunft* ended up contributing to a major anti-gay backlash which dominated public debate for months, putting the work of the SHC back years.[65] In the wake of this event, the German establishment went on the offensive, threatening to criminalise sex between women in 1910.

These divisions reflected fundamental problems inside the SPD to do with competing ideas about what kind of socialism was being fought for and the kind of struggle that needed to be waged to achieve it. It was a division that existed across the parties of the Second International and essentially pivoted on what Hal Draper has called the "two souls of socialism" – between those who saw socialism being delivered from above by an enlightened few versus those who saw it rising from below through the collective struggles of workers.[66] In Germany the SPD claimed to stand in the revolutionary tradition of Marx but years of building up membership and institutions within the existing system had fostered an increasingly reformist practice inside the SPD. Leading members Eduard Bernstein and Karl Kautsky argued for a gradualist approach to socialism that centred on getting socialists elected into parliament. This was compounded by a low level of struggle and strikes, during which the SPD "could neither infiltrate its way to corridors of power nor storm the buildings".

The creeping accommodation with capitalism, and the conservatism this generated, could be detected in even the best positions taken on sexual politics inside the SPD, as Noel Halifax notes:

> The SPD with its clubs and society within a society was firmly based on the respectable working class. The material basis of oppression – the family – was left uncriticised. The SPD was built within the structure of capitalist society, and one of its superstructures in which it was most deeply embedded was the nuclear family. The idea that fighting for sexual liberation meant a vision of socialism where the labels of heterosexual and homosexual would lose meaning, where the family would lose its importance and the separation between public and private lives would end, was a vision alien to most of the SPD.[67]

It also meant the party came to encompass a whole range of political opinion from reactionary to progressive and revolutionary. Thus Hirschfeld, on the right of the party, remained committed to a narrow approach of appealing to the great and the good for legal reform despite the central role of SPD members in supporting his cause. This approach not only proved to be incapable of achieving even the limited goal of repealing the anti-gay laws; it became subsumed by one of the biggest disasters in human history – the First World War.

The onset of war created a crisis across the left. Only two years previously the parties of the Second International had met and unanimously opposed war, but in 1914, with the exception of Russia and Belgium, they supported it. This line was followed by Hirschfeld, who could only respond to the prospect of the slaughter of millions of people in the trenches as follows:

> We must be and are of course prepared for any eventuality. What is necessary, however, is that the Committee be able to hold out and be there when – after what is hoped will be a quick, victorious end of the war – domestic efforts for reform are again stirred to activity, and when, therefore, the struggle for the liberation of homosexuals, too, picks up again.[68]

The capitulation of the left was a tragedy first and foremost for the millions of people slaughtered on the front. But it also dragged back the struggles of all progressive movements and organisations from homosexual rights to the trade unions.

The ruling class mobilised the whole economy behind the war machine. As Chris Harman notes, "Forty years of slow improvement gave way to a nightmare of deterioration." In order to get the population behind the war effort, and limit dissent, patriotic fervour was whipped up on a massive scale and harsh sedition laws introduced which assaulted civil liberties. The pressure to suspend the struggle was huge. Trade union and socialist leaders acquiesced to it with their "social truce". The war drained Germany of its activists and created massive confusion on the left. It is estimated around half of SHC activists were sent to the front and membership of the SPD and trade unions fell by 50 percent.[69]

As the war dragged on, death in trenches and hunger at home began to generate discontent. Marches for bread and arguments against the war began to come together. A mood of rebellion was brewing across Europe, but it was in Russia, not Germany that it was to break out.

Russia 1917 – a festival of the oppressed

The October 1917 Russian Revolution was a revolt against war, tyranny and want, but it was also to usher in an unprecedented advance in the struggle for sexual liberation.

Early 20th century Russia seemed an unlikely place for the zenith of homosexual liberation. It was an incredibly poor, unequal and repressive semi-feudal country, ruled by an autocratic tsar. The vast majority of people lived a brutal existence on the land in small isolated communities dominated by the local lord, church and a sexual conservatism. Women had few rights. Husbands were legally entitled to beat their wives. Sodomy was punishable by exile and forced labour in Siberia. The law was silent on lesbianism and even the notion of homosexuality was alien to the vast majority of people outside the big urban centres.

But parts of the country were also undergoing rapid industrialisation and in some of the big cities people were beginning to explore new opportunities for sexual experiences and relationships outside of the bounds of old familial ties and forms of social control which stretched back centuries. In 1907 for example, a critic of the time could refer to "the little homosexual world" of St Petersburg, which embraced bath houses, balls, parties and cruising areas in parks and other public spaces. Many of these public activities were only possible for men, but women too found opportunities to explore their sexuality in a range of settings from the friendship "circle" of wealthy women to lesbian women who dressed and lived as working men.

This gay subculture was developing in the context of harsh conditions of poverty, exploitation and the spread of market relations into growing areas of life. Two of the areas where same-sex relationships between women are most documented are among prostitutes and in prisons. Many of the liaisons between men took the form of upper class men paying for sex from their "subordinates" – workers and soldiers looking to supplement their income. In some of the bath houses sophisticated prostitution rings existed. However, outside of these money transactions, it seems people did find pleasure in same-sex intimacy and sometimes chose to live together.

New ideas about sexuality were given a boost by an attempted revolution in 1905, which although unsuccessful, gave confidence to those calling for reform of the law. The relaxation of censorship that followed the revolution also opened up a space in which new ideas about sexuality could be discussed. But there was nothing resembling the gay movement or modern gay consciousness evident in Germany.

Despite this one of the first acts of the new revolutionary workers' government of 1917 was the decriminalisation of homosexuality as part of an attempt to free people's lives from the tyranny of old laws and superstitions. They also made marriage an easy registration process, granted divorce on request, replaced the age of consent with the concept of sexual maturity and ended the different legal status of illegitimate children. Abortion was also legalised in 1920.

The leading Bolshevik Gregorii Batkis in his 1923 pamphlet *The Sexual Revolution in Russia* explained:

> The revolution is important not only as a political phenomenon which secures the political role of the working class, but also for the revolutions which evolving from it reach into all areas of life… [Soviet legislation] declares the absolute non-involvement of state and society in sexual relations provided they harm no one and infringe upon on no one's interests.[70]

This idea that neither the church nor the state should interfere in sexual matters was at the time a very modern one. But what made it revolutionary was its connection to a practical struggle by millions of people to uproot all of the structures of oppression, and to mobilise society's resources in a way that would give everybody genuine choices about their personal lives and sexual relationships.

Central to that struggle was an attempt to undermine the family's role as a prison house for women and source of sexual oppression. But this could not be done simply by decree. As Trotsky, a leading figure in the revolution, and commander of the Red Army responsible for defending revolutionary gains, argued:

> A radical reform of the family and more generally of the whole order of domestic life requires a great conscious effort on the part of the whole mass of the working class, and presumes in the class itself a powerful molecular force of inner desire for culture and progress. A deep going plough is needed to turn up heavy clods of soil.[71]

Women's role in achieving radical reform of the family was to be key. Strikes organised by women had been the spark for the February Revolution that toppled the tsar and initiated the movement towards workers' power in October. Lenin argued that their participation at every level, from the workplace to political leadership, should continue to "be the yardstick of the revolution". A department of women, the Zhenotdel, was set up to campaign for women's rights. Work was done to equip women with the basic skills of literacy and numeracy they needed to lead independent lives. Propaganda trains and ships were sent to remote areas to promote a message of equality using art, dance, film and theatre. Collective childcare and communal dining rooms were organised to release women from the drudgery of the home. Prostitution was decriminalised and co-operatives organised to house the women who had worked as prostitutes, providing medical support, training and alternative jobs. Everyone was encouraged to participate as equal citizens in a society geared towards collectively meeting human need.

These steps were also to be the groundwork for the creation of new sexual relations which Alexandra Kollontai, leading Bolshevik and Commissar for Social Welfare, argued would be "purified of all material elements, of all money consideration".[72]

In her many pamphlets on the family and free love she showed how in class society, our sexual relationships are distorted by private property, inequality and want. The idea of private property extended to seeing women as men's property in marriage, and generated jealousy and possessiveness in all personal relations. Inequality undermined the basis for equal relationships and want bound people to unhappy relationships through the various ties of necessity and survival. Thus:

> one of the constant features of social struggle has been the attempt to challenge relationships between the sexes and the types of moral codes that determine these relationships; and the way personal relationships are organised in a certain social group has had a vital influence on the outcome of the struggle between hostile social classes.[73]

The importance accorded to such matters was a reflection of the new horizons being opened up by the revolution which spanned everything from the commanding heights of industry to the problems of everyday life. It was a process that saw some of the most oppressed groups in society – women, the young, Jews and oppressed nationalities – come to the fore. This was no less true of homosexuals.

Historian Dan Healey describes how many "post-1917 Soviet sources...suggest that self-identified homosexuals in Russia believed the revolution had ended the state's refusal of the private" for same-sex relations, licensing their right to love.[74] "There was a sense there that gay people saw this as their revolution too. I can think of one drag queen in Kursk, written about in a medical article, who really does seem to interpret the events of the civil war and revolution as a licence to be quite flagrant and outrageous".[75]

Two women who had married secretly before the revolution had their marriage recognised, 88 years before civil partnerships were introduced in Britain. One of the women involved, Evgeniia Fedorovna, later argued for acceptance of "same-sex love…no longer oppressed or smothered by [our] own lack of consciousness and by petty bourgeois disrespect".[76]

The new Communist government made links with Hirschfeld's Institute and sent delegates to the International Congresses of the World League for Sexual Reform in Berlin (1921), Copenhagen (1928), London (1929) and Vienna (1930), where Russia was held up as a model for world sexual reform.[77]

The new freedom in the way people in Russia could express their sexual lives was part of a greater social revolution led by the working class. It was in a very real sense what Engels had envisaged to be "a festival of the oppressed".

In that struggle to fit the world anew, the Bolshevik Party fought to apply some of the best socialist traditions on sexual liberation. The utopian socialists had dreamt of a new society where human beings would create relationships based on love and comradeship. In Russia workers' power created a foundation for a real-life experimentation in these matters. Socialists from the earliest had challenged the institution of the family and linked women's and sexual oppression to the wider subjugation of one class by another. The Russian Revolution saw a heroic fight to uproot the family institution and free gender and sexual relations from the "cage bars" that bound them. In Germany, the SPD played a key role in supporting the first gay movement in the world. The

Bolsheviks made links with that movement and became internationally recognised for their contribution to sexual liberation.

All of this required a huge stuggle. Revolution is not a one-day event, but a process. The old does not uniformly or immediately give way to the new. This is particularly the case with women's oppression and sexual restrictions that are rooted in structures and prejudices that stretch back centuries and are intimately bound up with our most personal feelings. As Trotsky argued, in politics and economics the working class has the capacity to act "as a whole" and is often driven to do so by the pressures of exploiation. In "domestic life", however, "the working class is split into cells constituted by families". In Russia, where at least 80 percent of the population still lived in small isolated rural communities, Trotsky could complain that even at the height of the revolution there was "more than a little of the foul old leftovers of serfdom in the field of personal morals, the family and everyday life". [78]

The difficulties involved in constructing a new world were shaped by horrendous conditions of economic collapse, famine and war that left the revolution fighting for its life. The basic premise of socialism is that liberation from oppression can only be achieved if the material conditions exist to build a society without class inequality. The economic backwardness of Russia meant that spreading the revolution to more advanced economies such as Germany was essential. But in the meantime, the new workers' democracy faced a civil war with the old regime and a major assault by the global capitalist class, which ordered 14 armies to invade. These battles sucked away people and resources from the revolution. It meant that even some of the newfound personal freedoms people enjoyed had contradictory effects. Family break-ups could be liberating for those involved, but in the context of extreme hardship family members could find themselves left behind struggling to survive.

This didn't stop people from fighting for radical change and the Bolsheviks were even attacked in the international press for their supposed moral degradation. During one interview with an American journalist Trotsky famously responded to a question about whether it was true that divorce on demand was available in Russia by asking whether it was true that it wasn't in other countries. However, the conditions of civil war and famine placed very real limits on the fight by the Bolsheviks to revolutionise all areas of life.

What the Bolsheviks were able to achieve was also shaped by the particular context of Russia where, unlike Germany, a homosexual identity had barely emerged, never mind a movement. This meant a tradition of debate and struggle around these questions had not developed in Russia in advance of the revolution. Even Alexandra Kollontai, who was the most prolific writer on sexual matters, never talked explicitly about same-sex relationships. We cannot know how that might have changed had the revolution, and the new sexual freedoms introduced, been able to run their course. As Kollontai once explained, "the justification that I live by the new morality doesn't help anyone since the new morality is still only in the process of being formed".[79]

Despite this the Bolsheviks and the Russian Revolution put the achievement of genuine sexual liberation on the political and historical agenda. They started from a position which was opposed to any state, religious or "moral" interference into sexuality and sexual relationships in the context of leading a revolution deeply committed to liberation for all. The decriminalisation of homosexuality, recognition of marriage between people of the same sex and shaping of a climate in which trans and homosexual people could feel free to express themselves all flowed from this. It is why the Bolsheviks were to able to leapfrog over the achievements of

THE RED IN THE RAINBOW

the first homosexual movement in Germany – which was still struggling to repeal anti-gay laws – to win international recognition for being the most advanced country in the world on sexual rights. In the process they achieved a set of radical changes that can still inspire activists today.

Revolutionary hope in Germany

The new workers' democracy in Russia was a beacon for workers and the oppressed across the world who were desperate for an end to war and bitterly angry at the regimes which had sent them to pointless slaughter. In early 1918 a high-ranking American diplomat was to confide, "Bolshevism is gaining ground everywhere… We are sitting upon an open powder magazine and some day a spark may ignite it".[80] In Germany that spark was a sailors' mutiny in Kiel. Thousands of workers struck in their support, turning the town into a storm centre of rebellion, and a sailors' council was established. The dam had burst – sailors, soldiers and workers spilled onto the streets of Bremen, Hamburg, Hanover, Cologne, Leipzig and Dresden, finally reaching Berlin on 9 November 1918. The Kaiser fled, the war was ended and a republic based on universal suffrage declared. Workers' and soldiers' councils sprang up across the country.

Hirschfeld pointed to the impact of these struggles on sexual liberation: "The events of the year of 1918 had a certain effect on the liberation struggles of the homosexuals… Far beyond the groups of scientists, homosexual organisations have arisen…and taken up the struggle for their fellows".[81]

The SHC "took the most active part in all the revolutionary events" and the day the Kaiser abdicated, Hirschfeld spoke to a mass rally outside the Reichstag in which he called for a "social republic" in place of "racism and chauvinism": "Socialism means: solidarity, community, mutuality, further development of society into a unified body of people. Each for all and all for each!" He then paid tribute to "the great pioneers Lassalle, Marx, Engels, Bebel, Liebknecht, Singer and Jaurès".[82]

A delegation to the new government demanded the release of all homosexual prisoners. The renewed confidence among reformers generated by the revolution was reflected in attempts to form a "united front" of homosexual groups in Germany to take the struggle forward. Its Action Committee even wrote in the language of Marx and the international workers' movement as it declared, "In the final analysis you yourselves must win your rights. Justice for you will finally be the fruit of your efforts alone. The liberation of homosexuals can only be the work of homosexuals themselves".[83]

An Institute for Sexual Science was established which Hirschfeld fondly called the "child of the revolution". A banner headline of a 1920 publication from the Community of the Autonomous read, "Uranians of the World Unite!" Hirschfeld went on to set up the World League for Sexual Reform in 1921. This was followed by a series of international speaking tours including the 1922 Dutch tour which saw 900 people attend a meeting at The Hague and more than 2,000 in Vienna with hundreds turned away.[84] Other initiatives included the production of the first homosexual rights film *Different from Other People*.

Weimar Germany and in particular Berlin opened up the prospect of a homosexual subculture becoming more public than it ever was before. Its radical atmosphere attracted gays and others from across the world. Stefan Zweig wrote that "along the entire Kurfürstendamm powdered and rouged young men sauntered…and in the dim lit bars one might see government officials and men of finance tenderly courting drunken sailors without any shame". The French diplomat Ambois Got talked of the city as "a mad whirl of pleasure, a wild rush to enjoyment".[85] Homosexual groups and publications flourished. A homosexual theatre group, Theatre des

Eros, started up in 1921 with a programme including Christopher Marlowe's *Edward II* and a play about a woman who leaves her family for a lesbian relationship.

But the "gayest city in Europe" rested on very precarious conditions. It was, indeed, a child of the 1919 revolution, but by the summer of 1920 the great upsurge of struggle that created it had stalled. Another revolutionary wave in 1923 also failed to break through. In the wake of these massive defeats a growing volatility and political polarisation developed in the underbelly of Germany's "golden twenties".

The SPD played a shameful role in these events. Its votes in the German parliament had sent millions to the slaughter of the First World War trenches. When workers across Germany began to revolt against this insanity and establish workers' control of society, the SPD government mobilised a mercenary force, the Freikorps, to murder them in their thousands. Rosa Luxemburg and Karl Liebknecht, leaders of the Communist Party (KPD), were assassinated. The Freikorps later attempted a coup and were to become an early thuggish core of Hitler's Nazi Party.

In this battle Hirschfeld stood firmly with the right of the SPD, with the SHC going so far as to congratulate Friedrich Ebert – the man who had played a central role in crushing the revolution – on becoming first president of the Republic in 1919.[86] This was both a betrayal of the great hopes Hirschfeld had expressed for the future of socialism on the steps of the Reichstag, and a serious miscalculation in terms of the negative impact it would have on the struggle for homosexual rights. Now in government, the reformist SPD retreated from its pre-war position on homosexual rights and played a much more dubious role, agreeing in 1919 to legislation which set the penalty for sex between men at five years.

During the period the mantle of radical sexual politics passed over to the KPD, who in keeping with the revolutionary socialist tradition called on the "working class to show solidarity with all victims of a ruling class seeking to control it" – including homosexuals. A number of KPD members, such as Felix Halle and Wilhelm Reich, took up leading roles inside the SHC, as well as Richard Linsert, and developed very clear arguments for why the working class movement should support homosexual rights:

> The class-conscious proletariat, uninfluenced by the ideology of property and freed from the ideology of the churches, approaches the question of sex life and also the problem of homosexuality with a lack of prejudice afforded by an understanding of the overall social structure… In accordance with the scientific insight of modern times, the proletariat regards these relations as a special form of sexual gratification and demands the same freedom and restrictions for these forms of sex life as for intercourse between the sexes.[87]

Despite its strong support from the left, however, leading members of the SHC sought to play those links down. Kurt Hiller, the chair, argued, "The royalist must be just as welcome a helper as the socialist republican, the strict Catholic as welcome as the anarchist free thinker, the communist as the bourgeois democrat".[88] Of course there's nothing wrong with seeking unity over single issues with a broad range of forces, but the terms of that unity matter. In practice the SHC was pursuing a strategy which tailed the most right wing and reactionary social forces, undermining the effectiveness of the struggle.

This meant the SHC and many leading activists failed to take a position on the vital political questions that were emerging in Germany. It even tolerated Nazis in its ranks. In July 1927 after a Nazi speech in the Reichstag attacked homosexuality, the SHC put out the following statement: "We further feel obliged to urgently request of our numerous members in the National Socialist German Workers Party

[Hitler's party]…that they vigorously call their delegates to order".[89]

This polite approach to an organisation which had publicly celebrated the physical attacks on Hirschfeld, who had been shot at and on another occasion beaten up and left for dead because he was a Jewish homosexual, seems somewhat suicidal.

At the time the Nazis were regarded by many as a fringe organisation, and certainly not seen as a specific threat to homosexual people. The leader of their stormtroopers, Ernst Röhm, was a homosexual and the Hitler Youth had been nicknamed the Homo Youth. There was a lack of clarity generally on the left about the nature of Hitler's organisation and the kind of movement that was needed to confront it. The Russian revolutionary Trotsky was to develop a sharp analysis of both, but was in exile without the means to influence events on the ground. Meanwhile, the small organisation Hitler spent the 1920s systematically building was very suddenly to be catapulted onto the stage of history:

> The 1930s was a decade in which the forces of hope and despair fought on the streets of every city. It was a decade when revolution and counterrevolution were at each other's throats. It ended in a victory for counterrevolution which plunged the world into another war, accompanied by barbarities which put even the slaughter of 1914-18 in the shade.[90]

The rise of the Nazis

Germany was already experiencing an economic crisis when the Wall Street Crash dragged it down further in 1929. By 1932 industrial production had fallen by 42 percent and almost a third of workers were on the dole. Millions of middle class and small business people went into bankruptcy. The crisis gave a massive boost to the

Nazis. Their share of the national vote increased from 2.6 percent in 1928 to 18.3 percent in 1930, doubling to 37.1 percent in 1932. By that year it also had a street fighting force numbering 400,000.[91]

The Nazis' core support came from shopkeepers, small business people and the unemployed, whose social position left them isolated in the crisis. The fascist street mobilisations gave them a sense of power and order in a disintegrating world. The Nazis' attacks on "Jewish" and "alien" capitalism, or Bolshevism, appealed particularly to the rage of a petty bourgeoisie which felt squeezed between a strong working class movement and the power of big business. But as the crisis developed, sections of the ruling class began to see the Nazis as a means of breaking the power of the working class, and the key to restoring the profitability of the German economy.

In January 1933 Hitler was appointed chancellor. He moved quickly to liquidate militants who formed the backbone of working class and democratic organisations. Communist Party members were rounded up en masse and sent to camps; Kurt Hiller, who had welcomed members of Hitler's party into the SHC, was carted off to Oranienburg concentration camp; within six months all civil rights had been suspended, trade unions abolished, and a one-party state established.

The destruction of workers' organisations was combined with a Nazi ideology aimed at uniting the social classes as a nation. It glorified a mystical and mythical racial purity and the family. The scapegoats obstructing this golden age were Jews, the left, and homosexuals. Women were to be relegated to the role of mother and wife. Hitler regarded women's emancipation as a form of depravity.

Homosexual organisations were banned alongside working class organisations. Homosexuals were stigmatised, beaten and rounded up alongside Jews and socialists. The Nazis described Hirschfeld's Institute as "an unparalleled breeding ground of dirt and filth" and chose it for the first of many book burnings.

Paragraph 175 was extended to include nine offending acts including "a kiss, an embrace and a homosexual fantasy". Since it would be difficult for anyone to prove they were not having thoughts about homosexuality, this was a convenient premise to convict anyone seen as problematic to the regime. One man was arrested for allegedly watching a straight couple have sex in the park and convicted of only being interested in the man. Prosecutions shot up tenfold and second offenders were castrated. Having served their sentence, most gay men were interned in concentration camps. Homosexuals were purged from the Nazi Party and Röhm was killed in what became known as the "Night of the Long Knives". In 1937 the SS paper *Das Schwarze Korps* claimed that there were two million homosexuals in Germany and called for them to be interned.

Heinrich Himmler, the head of the Gestapo, described what they were doing to homosexuals as "merely the extinction of abnormal life. It had to be removed just as we pull up stinging nettles, toss them on a heap and burn them".[92]

The Nazis' terror was frighteningly modern and capitalist in its application. The biological categories of race and sexuality forged during the rise of industrial capitalism were systematised. The bedrocks of bourgeois society, the nation and the family, were taken to their extremes with eugenics aimed at defending the "purity of the race" and women ranked according to the number of children they had.

The logic of the industrial production line was applied to the concentration camps and the extermination of 11 million people.

The Nazis created a hierarchy even in the death camps. Jews, socialists, gays and other groups were marked out with different symbols; those for gay men (pink triangles) and lesbians (black triangles) were made one inch higher to signal their status as lowest of the low. Under "Project Pink":

the homosexuals were grouped into liquidation commandos and placed under triple camp discipline. That meant less food, more work, stricter supervision. If a prisoner with a pink triangle became sick, it spelled his doom. Admission to the clinic was forbidden.

Lesbians were forced to work in camp brothels where they were repeatedly raped. Gay men were slowly and painfully worked to death, as Holocaust survivor L D Classen von Neudegg was later to describe:

> All prisoners with the pink triangle...would be transferred as a unit to the Klinker Brickworks... Forced to drag along 20 corpses, the rest of us encrusted with blood, we entered... We had been here for almost two months, but it seemed endless years to us. When we were transferred here, we had numbered around 300 men. Whips were used more frequently each morning, when we were forced down into the clay pits under the wailing camp sirens. "Only 50 still alive," whispered the man next to me. "Stay in the middle – then you won't get hit so much".[93]

It is estimated that hundreds of thousands of lesbians and gays were murdered in the concentration camps.

The Holocaust was a catastrophe for humanity – a uniquely barbarous event in our history. It killed six million Jews and hundreds of thousands of other targeted groups. It destroyed the strongest and most developed workers' movement in the world. The vibrant homosexual subculture of Germany was consigned to the death camps.

Russia – the revolution betrayed

Lenin had warned, "Without the German revolution we are ruined." In the course of civil war, economic blockade and foreign invasion the material resources necessary for the revolution's survival were being drained away. At the same time the social force on which the workers' state rested, the working class, was being decimated – either killed fighting off foreign invasion and civil war or dragged away from the cities back into the countryside in search of food as the economy collapsed. This left the Bolshevik government running society in the name of a class that barely existed, and doing so in very difficult conditions. As early as 1920 Lenin had pointed out the problem: "Ours is a workers' state with bureaucratic distortions...borrowed from tsarism and hardly touched by the soviet world...a bourgeois and tsarist mechanism".[94]

A successful revolution in Germany would have mobilised fresh resources and class forces behind the workers' state in Russia. In the absence of that revolution, the conditions were created for counterrevolution and the rise of a new ruling class headed by Stalin. Trotsky, who formed the Left Opposition to Stalin during this period, put it like this:

> When there are enough goods in a store, the purchasers can come whenever they want to. When there are few goods, the purchasers are compelled to stand in line. When the lines are very long, it is necessary to appoint a policeman to keep order. Such is the starting point of the power of the Soviet bureaucracy.[95]

International revolution was abandoned in favour of what Stalin called "socialism in one country". The survival of Russia was no longer to be dependent on international revolution but on mobilising Russia's economy to match and take over its competitors and military rivals in the global capitalist economy. Its power was not to rest on workers' democracy but on a new ruling class who sought to achieve in decades what it had taken centuries for Western capitalism to achieve:

> There was the same use of force to drive the peasants from the land, the employment of child labour, and terror against those who might resist. Stalin carried through in a couple of decades what had taken 300 years to achieve in Britain. The result was a death toll enormously concentrated in time. The death toll in the labour camps was probably much lower than that of the Atlantic slave trade, but it took place over 25 years, not 250 years.[96]

Achieving such intense levels of exploitation required a break with every element of the revolution that had gone before. Every vestige of democracy and control was ripped away from ordinary people, millions were sent to prisons and labour camps, all political opposition was crushed. The break between the old gains and the new order was nowhere truer than in the field of sexual relationships. In 1933 homosexuality was made a crime once more and gay men sent to prison camps; motherhood was glorified with medals being awarded; and in 1936 abortion was criminalised.

Underlying these measures was the central importance of the family to a new ruling class which needed a rapidly expanded, healthy labour force. But as Trotsky pointed out, "The most compelling motive of the present cult of the family was undoubtedly the need of the bureaucracy for a stable hierarchy of relations." The new regime needed a new moral order around which to build its support, and scapegoats to persecute. Homosexuals were attacked as spies, fascists and bourgeois deviants – a cruel and disgusting slur given gays were being murdered at the hands of the Nazis during this period.

The horrific treatment of gays in Stalinist Russia was the product of the defeat of the revolution, and the restoration of capitalism. But the attempts by millions to shape a world free from such horrors, even in the most desperate conditions, is something that we should never lose sight of. As Victor Serge has said:

> It is often said that "the germ of all Stalinism was in Bolshevism at its beginning". Well, I have no objection. Only, Bolshevism also contained many other germs, a mass of other germs, and those who lived through the enthusiasm of the first years of the first victorious socialist revolution ought not to forget it. To judge the living man by the death germs which the autopsy reveals in the corpse – and which he may have carried in him since his birth – is that very sensible?[97]

In Russia and Germany the success of the struggle for sexual liberation was inextricably tied up with the fortunes of the radical left and the wider working class movement. When the working class movement reached its height by taking power in Russia, advances for sexual liberation reached their pinnacle. But when those forces were crushed under the boots of Stalin and Hitler, it also had devastating consequences for all the fantastic gains that had been won for homosexual rights.

Millions of people were killed in those defeats and with them the memory of the revolution as the festival of the oppressed was almost completely destroyed.

Tragically many on the left accepted the Stalinist characterisation of homosexuality as a bourgeois deviance. As a result of the Russian Revolution, the Bolshevik Party had towering stature around the world. Amid the horrors of the 1930s, people striving for an alternative to fascism and war also looked to Russia, often ignorant of many of the abuses taking place. This created a situation in which it was left to a small number of isolated individuals to try to uphold the genuine socialist tradition of sexual liberation.

Gay Liberation Front poster

4: The Stonewall riots and the birth of the new movement

On the night of 27 June 1969 a riot took place that changed the lives of LGBT people forever. It began with a police raid on the Stonewall Inn in Greenwich Village, New York – an underground bar frequented by working class lesbians and gays, many of them transvestites, prostitutes, and Hispanic and black people. They were regarded as the lowest of the low, accustomed to this kind of harassment and victimisation. But that night they fought back. The police were forced to barricade themselves in the bar and a three-day riot ensued:

> Graffiti calling for Gay Power had appeared along Christopher Street. Knots of youth – effeminate, according to most reports – gathered on the corners, angry and restless. Someone heaved a sack of wet garbage through the window of the patrol car. On nearby Waverly Place a concrete block landed on the hood of another police car that was quickly surrounded by dozens of men, pounding its doors and dancing on its hood… trash fires blazed, bottles and stones flew through the air, and cries of "Gay Power!" rang in the streets as police numbering 400 did battle with a crowd estimated at 2,000.[98]

The riot continued for three days and nights, and after those events nothing would be the same again. The beat poet Allen Ginsberg, who visited Greenwich Village not long afterwards, commented, "The guys there were so beautiful – they've lost that wounded look".[99] Within days a new organisation, the Gay Liberation Front (GLF), had been launched. Its founding statement declared:

We are a revolutionary group of men and women formed with the realisation that complete sexual liberation for all people cannot come about until existing social institutions are abolished. We reject society's attempt to impose sexual roles and definitions of our nature. We are stepping out of these roles and simplistic myths. We are going to be who we are... Babylon has forced us to commit to one thing – revolution.[100]

News of the riot spread around the world, and before long similar organisations had been launched in France, Canada, Australia, Germany, Italy, Belgium, Holland and Britain.

The Stonewall Inn, a blacked-out, dingy place which admitted its customers through a latchkey door, seemed an unlikely venue for the birth of the modern gay liberation movement. Like many other gay bars of the time it operated under the protection of a mafia racket whereby cash was paid over to police in order stop it from being shut down for violating city regulations. This did not stop regular raids, which were supposed to "keep up appearances" and formed part of a general ritual humiliation of lesbians and gays in American society. Not only did such raids bring arrests, beatings and even rape, they often attracted widespread publicity, with the names and addresses of those involved printed in the local papers. This very public outing often destroyed people's lives leading to them being sacked from jobs and shunned by family and friends.

Gay in 1950s America

Such harsh consequences were a reflection of the widespread oppression faced by lesbians and gays in American society. Homosexuality was illegal in all but one US state, carrying punishments of life imprisonment, internment in mental asylums and even castration. In 1954 a judge in Sioux City had used the newly introduced "sexual psychopath" laws to order the internment of all known homosexuals in the locality, leading to 29 men being carted off to asylums. During the same period, the government purge of political militants from unions and workplaces, which became known as the McCarthyite witch-hunts, also targeted lesbians and gays, who were designated as "perhaps as dangerous as communists". A Senate report into "sexual perverts" warned employers that "one homosexual can pollute a whole office" and thousands of lesbians and gays were driven out of their jobs or barred from federal employment.

The government drive against lesbians and gays encouraged widespread persecution, such that a survey in the 1950s found that 20 percent of gay men had suffered some form of harassment from the police.[101] It also generated a fear of gays in society as a mortal threat to the security and moral fabric of the nation. Even the film industry's code prohibited any portrayal of homosexuality until 1961. These stereotypes mixed with other prevailing ideas, such as those held by the medical establishment, which designated homosexuality as a sickness on a par with paedophilia.

This view of the homosexual as someone to be both pitied and feared, in need of a cure, but also deserving of punishment, continued into the 1960s. In the same year as the Stonewall riots, for example, *Time* magazine could carry the following review of a play dealing with homosexuality:

Homophile activists contend that there would be more happy homosexuals if society were more compassionate, still, for the time being at least, there is a savage ring of truth to the now famous line from *The Boys in the Band*: Show me a happy homosexual, and I'll show you a gay corpse.[102]

In this climate, lesbians and gays not only lived with the reality of discrimination but the terror and fear at being discovered and exposed. Worse still was the internalisation of these ideas. Many gays and lesbians sought treatments including electric shock therapy, hysterectomy and castration, in the hope that it would cure them. A gay man writing under the pseudonym Donald Webster Cory in the late 1940s pointed out in his seminal book, *The Homosexual in America*, that "the worst effect of discrimination has been to make the homosexuals doubt themselves and share in the general contempt of the sexual invert".[103]

Even organisations dedicated to improving the situation for lesbians and gays often ended up bowing to many of these prejudices.

The Mattachine Society had started out in 1950 with a very radical outlook on gay rights declaring "the heroic objective of liberating one of our largest minorities from social persecution".[104] This view of gays as a persecuted group, rather than a collection of unfortunate individuals, was groundbreaking for its time and reflected the politics of its founders, a group of left radicals drawn together by former Communist Party (CP) member Harry Hay. Although the CP in America persisted with the Stalinist slur which dismissed homosexuality as a "bourgeois deviance", it had a very good record on fighting racism and other injustices. Hay, who was gay himself, was able to apply these traditions to the oppression of gays and lesbians. The society focused its goals on investigating the roots of homosexual oppression and winning change by mobilising lesbians and gays into a movement which had "pride in belonging" to "the homosexual minority".[105]

Yet this radical approach very quickly came under fire from other activists who feared it would make Mattachine a target of the state's witch-hunts and undermine their ability to gently persuade those in power to accept them. Following the resignation of Mattachine's founding members, a very different approach was developed by the new leadership which centred on "aiding established and recognised scientists, clinics, research organisations and institutions" to encourage a better understanding of homosexuality in society.[106] The original emphasis on encouraging self-activity and pride among gays and lesbians was abandoned. Instead members were encouraged to develop a "pattern of behaviour that is…compatible with the recognised institutions…of home, church, and state" in order to avoid alienating potential support. Conformity was seen as the gateway to winning social acceptance. Collections for hospitals were organised to prove that homosexuals were "good citizens" and a campaign to repeal anti-sodomy laws was dropped for fear it might provoke a backlash.

A similar line was followed by the Daughters of Bilitis (DOB), the first lesbian political organisation, founded in 1955. Having started out as a social club aimed at breaking down the isolation faced by many lesbians, DOB broadened its scope to "encourage women to take an ever increasing part in the…fight for understanding of the homophile minority". But it too focused attention on the search for allies within the establishment such that even those with hostile ideas on homosexuality were invited to speak at DOB chapters and write in their magazine *Ladder*. In one instance members of the San Francisco chapter had to endure a guest speaker who told them, "the lesbian is unfulfilled and hampering her health and happiness".[107] In the pursuit of winning respectable opinion and social acceptance, lesbians were called on to do everything they could to integrate themselves into society. Women were encouraged to leave the bar scene with its butch/femme culture, while a transvestite attending a DOB convention was persuaded to wear "feminine" attire.

It took enormous courage to risk harassment, raids, public disgrace and criminalisation to build organisations and develop publications aimed at winning improvements for lesbians and gays. But the defensive, apologetic approach reflected the huge pressures faced by those prepared to do so and the immensely damaging impact of McCarthyism. As the 1960s wore on growing numbers of activists demanded a more radical response. In 1965, for example, the Mattachine branch in Washington passed a controversial motion stating, "Homosexuality is not a sickness, disturbance, or other pathology in any sense." These were early indications of the winds of change to come but also how far the gay movement had to go.

For all these reasons, the Stonewall riots astounded the world, and the movement that flowed from them represented a landmark in the birth of a new politics that demanded gay liberation. At the time the riots appeared to come out of the blue, but they were the product of a number of things coming together.

The winds of change

The Second World War had disrupted a lot of the old values and certainties central to US capitalism. The structures of family life and rigid role of the sexes in society were thrown up in the air as men were sent off to war and women went out to work in their millions. Those who were already married found themselves separated from partners and home life, while many single men and women sidestepped the well-trodden path from family home into married life to join the armed forces or war industries. Women whose horizons had been limited to their roles as wives and mothers were now confronted with mass media images of their sex marching into factories, wearing overalls and brandishing "V for Victory" signs, which emphasised their central contribution to the economy and war effort. Work bought with it a new financial independence and a very different social life centred in the big cities.

These developments opened up new opportunities for

people to explore and experience sexual and emotional relationships outside of the confines of marriage. In conditions of war, which cast doubt over the future and made life feel temporary, there was also a greater willingness to experiment. Some men and women who had same-sex experiences during the war returned home to marriages or heterosexual relationships, while others became aware of feelings and desires that might otherwise have gone unexplored. In the armed services lesbians and gay men could begin to identify each other with relative ease, and in the cities surrounding the war industries and port areas in New York, San Francisco and Los Angeles a lesbian and gay subculture grew.

In the years following the war those in power sought to push back many of these changes. Women who wanted to stay in their jobs were replaced by men returning from military service. Government propaganda and popular culture pumped out a mass of stereotypes which put domestic life and traditional male and female roles at its centre. A cover story in *Life* magazine in 1956 asserted that "of the accomplishments of the American woman, the one she brings off with the most spectacular success is having babies".[108] The McCarthyite witch-hunts against communists, homosexuals and other "enemies within" were part of a drive to suppress dissenting voices and impose a new stultifying conformity on society. All of this served to clamp down on the period of sexual experimentation that had taken place during the war.

However, in the longer term the economic boom continued to draw growing numbers of women into the workplace and higher education, and built up the cities, creating counterpressures to the ruling class's attempts to get things under their control. Women's greater economic independence and people's changed expectations about their right to enjoy fulfilling sex lives contributed to the loosening of ties between sex, marriage and having children. The popularity of the Kinsey Reports, which revealed widespread homosexual experiences, infidelity and sex before marriage, was one small reflection of this. When the pill finally became available to single as well as married women in the early 1970s this also gave women further control over their bodies and sexual choices.

At the same time some lesbians and gays were trying to build on the new possibilities they had experienced during the war. Their decisions to remain in the big cities rather than returning to home towns and families continued to shape a growing subculture. This found expression in the growth of literature dealing with gay and lesbian themes, and went alongside occasional press reports, features and "exposés" unearthing what was described as a bizarre and exotic underworld. Although much of this publicity was negative it contributed to widening public discussion about a group of people who had previously been barely acknowledged, even informing isolated individuals about where they could go to find this world.

In Britain the ruling class was forced to respond to these conflicts by trying to redraw a new consensus in a way that would preserve its overall interests. This involved both making concessions and sharpening persecution. A series of high-profile trials of homosexuals generated fears about the effectiveness of current laws in policing gay men. A new act was introduced in 1967 which legalised sex between men over the age of 21 in private at the same time as prosecutions for other homosexual offences were stepped up. But concessions like these emboldened people to fight for more and certainly inspired activists in the US.

1968 – seizing the time

The clash between the old and the new experienced by lesbians and gays was one element in much deeper contradictions which were helping to fuel movements for civil rights, women's liberation and an end to the Vietnam War.

Many black people had also returned from the war only to be confronted with the same old racist violence and institutionalised segregation. Their resistance to this had sparked a mass movement for civil rights in the South, which boiled over into an increasingly militant struggle in the North. Their success in fighting back had already begun to influence some of the activists arguing for a more radical approach in the homophile movement. The same Mattachine member who moved the motion opposing the view that homosexuality was a sickness had argued that black people:

tried for 90 years to achieve his purposes by a programme of information and education. His achievements in those 90 years, while by no means nil, were nothing compared to those of the past ten years, when he tried a vigorous civil liberties and social action approach... I do not see the NAACP and CORE worrying about which chromosome gene produced a black skin or about the possibility of bleaching the Negro... We are interested in obtaining rights for our respective minorities, AS Negroes, AS Jews and AS HOMOSEXUALS. Why we are Negroes, Jews or homosexuals is totally irrelevant, and whether we can be changed to whites, Christians or heterosexuals is equally irrelevant.[109]

The year before the Stonewall riots, 1968, had seen this revolt come together in a way that put revolution on the agenda. This centred on events in France, where the biggest general strike in history caused the president to flee the country for an army base in Germany. Here he confided to the generals, "Everything is fucked. The communists have provoked paralysis across the whole country. I'm in charge of nothing."

In the US the legitimacy of capitalism was already being torn apart by the Vietnam War and the state's violent attacks on civil rights marchers. 1968 started with a mass Vietnamese peasant uprising against occupying troops which brought home to the world that the US could not win the war. The assassination of Martin Luther King followed not long after and was met with riots involving tens of thousands of people. The world's other empire, Russia, also found itself under siege from Czechoslovakia to Poland and Yugoslavia where resistance was growing to the "red bourgeoisie". This created a crisis not only for those regimes, but also for so-called Communism itself, as the decision by Moscow to send tanks into Czechoslovakia to crush dissent began to break people's illusions that those societies were genuinely socialist. From East to West the status quo was under attack. The revolt even entered the Olympic Games in Mexico that year when two black American athletes used the medal ceremony to raise the Black Power salute.

The modern gay movement was inspired and influenced by these events. The chant "Gay Power" echoed the chants of "Black Power" which had rung through many cities in the riots that followed Martin Luther King's assassination. When the GLF formed it named itself after the National Liberation Front – the resistance movement fighting US troops in Vietnam. One of its first acts was a call for solidarity with the imprisoned Black Panther leader Huey P Newton. It very quickly got involved in the wider movement and took part in a wide range of protests and demonstrations.

In their founding statement, the GLF members showed themselves to be part of a struggle to transform the entire world and called for revolution. When asked what revolution meant, they answered:

> We identify ourselves with all the oppressed; the Vietnamese struggle, the third world, the blacks, the workers, all those oppressed by this rotten, dirty, vile, fucked up capitalist conspiracy.

This marked a radical departure from the defensive, reformist approach that had dominated the homophile organisations in the 1940s and 1950s – the term homophile had been chosen by activists because it avoided reference to anything sexual. Where they had attempted to win liberal opinion to an acceptance of gays, the GLF asserted gay pride. In place of the focus on lobbying institutions to support them, they called for the mass involvement of gays, encouraging them to fight back "in a community numbering millions". The slogan "It's not me who's sick, but a society that calls me sick" summed up a rejection of everything that had gone before, and was linked to a serious attempt to identify the roots of gay oppression within the system. These people were out for revolutionary change and put forward a vision of sexual liberation, not just for lesbians and gays, but everyone: "new forms and relations…based upon brotherhood, cooperation, human love and uninhibited sexuality". The central involvement of trans people in the movement was an important factor in shaping a sexual politics that was about breaking in every way from the search for tolerance, in favour of a radical challenge with every aspect of the status quo, sexuality, gender and the rest. As trans activist Sylvia Rivera, who took part in the riots, put it:

We were not taking any more of this shit. We had done so much for other movements. It was time… All of us were working for so many movements at that time. Everyone was involved with the women's movement, the peace movement, the civil rights movement. We were all radicals. I believe that's what brought it around. I was a radical, a revolutionist… If I had lost that moment, I would have been kind of hurt because that's when I saw the world change for me and my people.

The GLF took the methods of the wider movement into the fight for gay liberation. Sit-ins were organised at establishments which refused to serve gays, bigoted politicians were hounded, homophobic newspapers had their offices occupied and picketed, the psychiatric establishment had their conferences disrupted, police raids on gay bars were met with demonstrations. Gays and lesbians brought a new flair to some of these activities, with dance-ins and kiss-ins organised in defiance of the law and police harassment. Alongside this a multitude of different gay organisations, campaigns and publications flourished.

Although many of these activities involved a relatively small number of people, the movement brought a new consciousness to millions of gay people around the world who had previously lived with fear, shame and humiliation. "Out of the closets, onto the streets" was one of the main slogans of the movement and the sense of liberation it brought was huge. As the GLF's paper *Coming Out* reported after the first Gay Pride in 1970, "These days mean something special for every lesbian and homosexual – they mark the first time that gays took to the streets, angry, proud, joyous – tearing down the prisons in which sexist society has chained us".[110]

This dramatic change in the way gays viewed themselves, along with the seismic shift in public opinion towards gays as a result of the struggles waged, was the historic contribution of the Stonewall riots and the movement that flowed from it. Important reforms were also won. In the US over half the states had repealed their anti-homosexual laws by the late 1970s and the Psychiatry Association, which had for over a century held homosexuality to be a mental illness, struck it off their books. In Britain little more was won in terms of legal changes, but the struggle helped to deliver a much greater openness for lesbians and gays.

The dream deferred

But the GLF's dream of a revolution that would bring real sexual liberation went unrealised. It had ceased to exist as an organisation in the US and Britain by 1973. So what happened?

Once again the gay liberation movement was intimately linked with a wave of revolt against the system, and in the beginning there was a great deal of optimism about what was possible. The GLF's slogan "Make a revolution – it's just a kiss away" summed this up. Yet as time wore on, those people who were fighting back had to confront the reality of a capitalist system which, although shaken, was not beaten.

In the US by the mid-1970s a number of victories had been won – America lost in Vietnam, segregation was on its way out and President Nixon resigned in the wake of the Watergate scandal. But people saw the power and brutality of the US state when four students were killed during anti-war protests at Kent State University in 1970. The black struggle had given a central impetus to the fightback in the US, but by this point many activists in the Black Panther party had been imprisoned or killed. The movements lost their momentum and direction. Some activists began to turn away from street politics as taking up positions within the existing institutions began to look like a more realistic option for achieving change in society.

In Britain an upward surge of strikes ousted a Tory government in 1974 and many people voted Labour in with high hopes. Yet within months of coming to power Labour responded to the onset of an economic recession by imposing a crippling wage freeze on workers in the form of the "social contract". Many leading trade union activists, including members of the CP, the biggest left organisation in Britain at the time, saw no alternative but to stand by "their" government. The result was an alliance of reformist politicians and trade union officials which demobilised a powerful working class movement, leaving groups of workers to wage bitter fights against the social contract in isolation from one another. This pattern was to be repeated in many other countries, including in Italy under "the historic compromise" and in Spain with "the social pact".

In this context political confusions and divisions inside the lesbian and gay movement began to matter a great deal.

From the beginning there were many divisions among activists about who they were fighting and what they were fighting for. Some wanted a radical change in lifestyle, others wanted to create a powerful gay bloc in official politics. Even those who called for revolutionary change had very different ideas about what that actually meant.

On these questions the revolutionary socialist tradition had a lot to offer, but the modern gay movement came with little knowledge of previous movements for gay liberation or the red thread that ran through them. As we have seen, the memory of socialist revolution and the pioneering work of socialists on the question of sexual liberation had largely been extinguished in the preceding decades.

The main organisations of the left, the Communist Parties, carried with them the Stalinised sexual politics which persisted with the view of homosexuality as a bourgeois deviance, expelled gay members and encouraged them to live "respectably". High-profile individuals on the left such as the historian Eric Hobsbawm had claimed there was no link between socialist revolution and sexual liberation, while French philosopher Michel Foucault rejected the French Communist Party in part because of its homophobia. Isolated Communist Party members and other small revolutionary organisations maintained something of the genuine socialist traditions of sexual liberation, but they were too small to overcome the dead weight of Stalinism. In the US Harry Hay had had to leave the CP in order to build the Mattachine

Society even as the state mobilised homophobia as part of their drive against the organised working class.

When people radicalised by the struggles of the 1960s were drawn to socialist politics, different versions of Stalinism remained influential. As they fought against war in Vietnam and racism at home, many looked to the inspiration of Cuba where a national liberation struggle had kicked out a US-backed dictator and was fighting to throw off the shackles of foreign domination in the wake of an economic blockade. In China too, Mao's "Cultural Revolution", which mobilised students against old Communist Party managers and bureaucrats as part of a campaign to drive up productivity, appeared to be involving large numbers of young people in a challenge to authority. For many people in the West they saw the calls for a cultural revolution and student protests but didn't understand the motor behind it.

In the context of the Cold War, countries which had led successful national liberation movements and used the rhetoric of socialism appeared to offer a very powerful alternative to US capitalism. In reality they had little to do with socialism. In Cuba the overthrow of Batista was a major victory against colonial oppression, but it was primarily a national liberation struggle, not a revolution aimed at radically reorganising society. The new state had sought to reappropriate its country's resources from foreign powers in the form of huge nationalisations, but that state continued to organise the economy on capitalist lines. A similar form of state capitalism existed in China and Russia. All of these regimes, faced with isolation from the world markets, sought to increase productivity not only through increased levels of exploitation, but by bolstering the family.

One consequence of this was the terrible persecution of gays. In Cuba, for example, thousands were rounded up into labour camps. This was something gays discovered for themselves as they joined many other activists in the 1960s to do solidarity work in Cuba only to find themselves subject to homophobic abuse and, when they protested, barred from re-entering the country. These stories were reported widely in the gay press.

Not surprisingly these events, and the sexual conservatism among the Stalinist left, generated a hostility towards the organised left among many gay activists. Even those associated with the left were cut off from a genuinely revolutionary tradition which had been built up over previous generations. If Russia, China and Cuba were really socialist, people asked, then why look to socialism for sexual liberation? Socialism and working class struggle, it seemed, was mainly about economic justice not sexual freedom.

This was particularly the case in the US, where the organised left and working class movement had been greatly weakened by McCarthyism. It meant that during a decade of unrest, there was never a generalised wave of industrial struggle across the US. And even when big strikes did take place, there was no organised network of socialists fighting to link them up with the wider movements. Instead the movement organised itself into separate interest groups from black power to student power. The working class was rejected as force for change in favour of other groups, be it the "third world" or "the unemployed". Those out for revolutionary change looked to alternative methods of struggle from the armed struggle to taking over the existing institutions, neither of which would ever be able to successfully take on and overthrow the world's superpower.

In Britain, where strike waves were a major feature of the discontent and the non-Stalinist left had more influence, the GLF did organise solidarity with the working class movement. They took their "Gay People on the March!" banner to mass demonstrations against the Tories' anti trade union laws. Despite being relegated to the back on one occasion by "less than enthusiastic" organisers, they persisted, joining pickets in support of the Pentonville Dockers who were imprisoned for defying these laws – and later released without charge. Campaigns were also organised in support of victimised lesbian and gay trade unionists.

The notion that lesbians and gays should be linking up their struggle with the labour movement was not embraced by everyone. In London the very different activities pursued by the East London GLF branch, which organised solidarity with working class resistance, and the Brixton Radical Faeries, who were more concerned with living out alternatives to a "straight society", were indicative of the kind of arguments that existed.

As the working class struggle went into retreat the Brixton approach became much more prominent – a process that was accelerated by the theory and politics that shaped the movement.

Missing the red in the rainbow

The GLF had called for a revolutionary struggle against a capitalist system that created gay oppression, but on the exact nature of the system, what kind of revolution would be needed, and where the power lay to achieve it, they were vague. The socialist argument that the central dynamic of capitalism is the exploitation of workers to accumulate profits, and that this is the engine of oppression, which can only be ended by a working class with the power to overthrow it did not have a very wide purchase. The family was often pointed to as the key institution in the oppression of lesbians and gays, but it was seen largely in terms of its ideological role in the perpetuation of sexist ideas. If it had a material foundation, this was seen to stem from the domination of men rather than the economic and political interests of the capitalist class:

The oppression of gay people starts in the most basic unit of society, the family. Consisting of the man in charge, a slave as his wife and their children on whom they force themselves as the ideal models… Women and gay people are both victims of the cultural and ideological phenomenon known as sexism. This is manifested in our culture as male supremacy and heterosexual chauvinism.[111]

The idea that men, rather than class, were the root of the problem was systematised in feminist theory, which provided the gay movement with much of its theoretical underpinning. Radical feminist Shulamith Firestone, for example, argued in her 1970 book *The Dialectic of Sex*, "the political oppression of women has its own class dynamic". By the end of the decade patriarchy theory, which held that women's oppression was a system of male domination, had become common sense for much of the movement.[112] It is easy to see why these ideas could take root as a logical response to the manifestations of women's oppression, such as sexist behaviour or comments from men. But as a theory it presented a cul-de-sac which could not provide an explanation of where the sexism or homophobia came from beyond blaming some kind of inherent biological drive by men or straight people to oppress others. This encouraged a focus on waging narrow struggles against the particular symptoms of oppression unconnected from the root cause.

This in turn fuelled separatist politics since people reasoned – why collaborate with those who were responsible for your oppression? Feminist organisations such as Redstockings argued that "liberating women has priority above every other idea", while the New York Radical Women declared, "We ask not if something is 'reformist', 'radical', 'revolutionary' or 'moral'. We ask: is it good for women or bad for women?"[113] Many of these women were reacting to sexism in the movement, but the theories and strategies they developed created splits between people who had been working together. In 1970 a group of women left the American GLF to form Radicalesbians. Their founding document *The Woman-Identified Woman* argued that women needed to break from male domination both in society and the movement.[114] The divisive nature of these ideas became clear in the 1980s when black lesbians and gays responded to racism by organising separately from their white counterparts. Bisexuals were also shunned for "sleeping with the enemy".

Without a strategy to win people away from prejudices through a common struggle our side will always be weak and divided and unable to take on the structures which perpetuate oppression. The GLF had won powerful allies for the gay struggle in the Black Panther movement because of the solidarity they organised for imprisoned activists. Some gay activists had argued against giving support because of homophobia among some Black Panthers, but where solidarity was built it was returned by one of the most respected leaders of the Black Panthers, Huey P Newton, who came out in support of gays:

Homosexuals are not given freedom and liberty by anyone in society. Maybe they might be the most oppressed people in the society. The terms faggot and punk should be deleted from our vocabulary and especially we should not attach names normally designed for homosexuals to men who are enemies of the people.

This was a powerful statement of support for gay liberation from a fighter who inspired millions across America, and around the world. But the rejection of this notion that people could and must be won from prejudiced ideas or behaviour in a struggle to change the world resulted in an atmosphere of blame and recrimination, where what mattered was who was the most oppressed.

Separatist politics contributed to a retreat into lifestyle and personal politics which stressed challenging oppression through personal relationships and lifestyle choices. Activists involved in the gay movement had always put a strong emphasis on personal politics with notions like "make a revolution in your life" and "the personal is political". For lesbians and gays who had lived life in the closet, or suffered the humiliations of homophobia, these ideas had a strong currency and a positive side, reflecting a sense of optimism about the possibility of creating immediate change.

Activists built gay communes or squats where people could live "a new liberated lifestyle which will anticipate as far as possible the free society of the future". People sought to live life outside of the family, challenge traditional gender roles and explore more liberated sexual relationships which broke with the possessiveness of monogamy. Consciousness-raising groups aimed at transforming the world by transforming people's minds. The problem was that these activities on their own had very little impact beyond the lives of those individuals involved. Most people couldn't drop out, because they had to find ways of surviving by getting whatever work they could. Squats and communes came up against the power of the landlords and the courts, or fell apart as people felt the pressure of trying to radically change their lifestyles in the absence of wider social change. Consciousness-raising often acted as an outlet for bitter personal experiences but failed to provide a stepping stone towards getting involved in the struggle.

The decline of the wider struggle and the influence of radical feminism and separatist politics shaped an increasingly inward-looking and moralistic approach. Lifestyle choices became a *substitute* for political action and without a set of ideas which anchored the problem of oppression in the organisation of society personal relationships became the main arena of struggle. Lesbians called on women to fight their oppression by rejecting men and converting to lesbianism. Some argued only lesbians and gay men could really challenge the sexist roles in society, while others also saw gay men as a problem because they celebrated male bonding and argued that they should subordinate their struggle to the women's movement. In the US, for example, a group of gay men who accepted these arguments formed the Flaming Faggots and dedicated their activity to living a life that was "unmanly without parodying women". They finally came to the conclusion that "androgyny would undermine the patriarchy and the revolution would ensue". In Britain a series of internalised arguments took place in which different groups were accused of selling out because of which group they belonged to or the lifestyle they led. A particularly bitter attack occurred against lesbians who engaged in S&M.

The original call for gay liberation had expressed a desire for a sexual liberation in which people could be free from the straitjacket of narrow choices and expectations but was now imposing a new set of limits and moral judgements on people's relationships. Coming out became a necessary precursor to being involved in the movement. This automatically excluded many people not yet confident enough to come out to their family, workmates or friends, particularly working class lesbians and gays for whom it was not so easy to escape to the scene with its bars, communes and alternative lifestyles. This represented a shift from the early days when emphasis was put on coming out collectively at demonstrations and on marches.

New gains and new challenges

Lifestyle and identity politics felt radical because it appeared to represent an immediate challenge to some of the most visible manifestations of oppression. However, the very success of the movement was opening up a space in society where people could begin to express their sexuality more openly without the structures of capitalism caving in. As early as the mid-1970s some activists were talking about the problem of incorporation as a small commercial gay scene began to develop:

> The closeted atmosphere of gay bars dissolved into gold dust as the proprietors realised they could allow gays to dance together without the (legal) heavens falling in... If gay liberation could set up a people's disco, so could Tricky Dicky. If gay liberation could publish gay magazines, so could Don Busby; bigger and glossier, if rather less liberated. Gay liberation prised open the crack, but gay commercial interests rushed to pour in. The result is that increasingly the gay world is moulded and defined explicitly by the values of capitalism.[115]

In reality the scene in the 1970s was tiny compared to the scale of the pink economy today, which makes billions selling everything from gay porn to weddings. It was also an important step forward that lesbians and gays began to lead more open lives; whether that involved going to a gay disco or buying gay magazines, it was hardly selling out! But there was a very important truth in what was being expressed.

The movement had begun by burning down an underground gay bar, and quite explicitly attacking a scene or "gay ghetto" which exploited the repressive environment faced by lesbians and gays. As the movement won greater openness it helped to generate gay venues, publications and services that had not existed before, and these came to be seen by some capitalists as something they could not only live with but also profit from.

This reflected the contradictory nature of some of the changes being won by the gay movement – new gains also bought new problems and challenges.

Another arena where a space began to open up was official politics, which had previously been closed off to lesbian and gay activists. In the US the initial approach of "zapping" politicians to force them to make positive statements about gays became a much more sophisticated process of targeting and lobbying key politicians and seeking to influence the national policy of the Democratic Party. By 1972 key gay activists were in leading roles campaigning for the Democratic Party and in 1977 the president invited the Gay Task Force into the White House.

In Britain the rise of the Tories and election of Margaret Thatcher, alongside a downturn in militant struggle, was accompanied by a growing movement to reshape the Labour Party into an organisation that could oppose the Tories and build resistance. This push to reforge a "mass socialist party" was fuelled by anger at the previous Labour government, which had presided over unemployment, vicious cuts and the first fall in real wages since the end of the war. As momentum for the project grew around the figure of Tony Benn, growing numbers of socialists and radicals who had been involved in the various movements joined the Labour Party in the conviction that it offered the most effective vehicle for achieving change. This seemed confirmed in the early 1980s when Tony Benn stood for deputy leadership on a left reformist ticket (only very narrowly losing) and the Labour left won control of a number of local councils including the Greater London Council (GLC), which became a focus for gay and lesbian activists who wanted to push forward gay rights. This seemingly forward march of the left and progressive politics inside the Labour Party, however, was to come up against some serious challenges.

The events of Stonewall and the movement it gave birth to had a huge impact and won fantastic gains for LGBT people. These gains continued to be felt at every level of society even as the highpoint of the struggle receded. However, they were being achieved in the context of capitalism restabilising itself. The vision raised by the Stonewall rioters, of a society where there was "complete sexual liberation for all people", was not realised. The revolution which would abolish "all existing social institutions" did not happen. The British GLF's warning that "reforms we might painfully extract from our rulers would only be fragile and vulnerable" seemed forgotten. For many lesbians and gays enjoying newfound freedoms, this did not seem so important. But it did place real limitations on the nature of the victories being won for our side. The retreat of the movement was also shaping a more narrow set of politics that would prove to be insufficient to confront the new attacks soon to come.

5: Thatcher, AIDS and the miners who marched on Gay Pride

After the 1960s the world would never be the same again. Significant victories had been won by millions of exploited and oppressed people around the globe and for a time the rich and powerful felt under siege. By the mid to late 1970s, however, the struggles which had driven these changes had faltered. Governments and big business systematically attempted to incorporate the unions and social movements into running a changed but still fundamentally unequal society.

The election of Thatcher in Britain and Reagan in the US reflected this situation. Shifting the balance of forces in society back in favour of the ruling class was central to their agenda. This would involve an attempt to break the power of organised workers and roll back the legacy of the 1960s. However, both Thatcher and Reagan inherited a situation in which their authority and forces were greatly weakened. They were also confronted with a new consensus in society which was much more favourable to the rights of black people, women and gays. This meant they had to be initially quite careful about who they attacked and how.

In Britain, where industrial struggle had been at the centre of resistance, the Tories pursued a strategy of breaking the most militant groups of workers one by one, avoiding an all-out assault. This involved making concessions to some workers while attacking others, and eventually culminated in a confrontation with one of the most organised groups of workers in Britain – the miners – who had caused the downfall of a Tory government in 1974. After a year-long strike they were defeated in 1985. The victories of workers in earlier decades had helped fuel confidence among lesbians and gays in the possibility of revolutionary change. Now their defeats shaped a very different climate in which lesbians and gays also found themselves under attack.

The right rebuilds

Both Thatcher and Reagan sought to build a new right wing consensus on social issues. This provided them with an ideological pole around which to attract a range of forces, while also fostering divisions among those they wanted to attack. In Britain, for example, the miners became the ultimate "enemy within", but a host of other social groups from single parents to "aliens" (migrants) had preceded them.

Even on this front, some of the attacks had to be coded. So Thatcher, rather than going for an all-out attack on women's or gay rights, talked about the importance of "family values" and the problem of single parents. But this created a fertile soil for maverick elements who were more explicit in their rhetoric against particular oppressed groups. In the US for example, a significant constituency had built up around the "Moral Majority" and religious right in the late 1970s, which provided large amounts of funding and crucial electoral support for Reagan in 1980. These groups spearheaded campaigns to push back gay and women's rights in the US, which, even though they didn't always lead to government action, helped to create a climate which made it easier for the right to push their agenda.

One major flashpoint in this struggle in Britain was the Tories' attacks on local Labour left councils. In the early 1980s Labour controlled more than 150 cities, towns and boroughs including London, Glasgow, Manchester, Birmingham, Liverpool, Sheffield, Newcastle, Leeds, Edinburgh and Bradford. Some were under the influence of the left as Labour Party activists who had been involved in the movements against gay and women's oppression and racism took up council positions. They were centres of strong workplace organisation, with council workers representing about 20 percent of all union membership at the time. The jewel in the crown of these "socialist town halls" was the GLC, which saw Ken Livingstone, or "Red Ken" as he became known, elected in 1981 with a million Labour votes.

The progressive policies of the GLC and left Labour councils made them a rallying point for those who hated what Thatcher represented. At a time when the Tories were seeking to cut services and redistribute wealth in favour of the rich, the councils pledged "no cuts, no rent rises and no rate rises". The GLC slashed public transport fares under their "Fares Fair" policy and agitated against mass unemployment, which had been one of the sparks for a series of inner city riots in 1981 – constructing a huge sign on top of their building opposite parliament which showed the rising unemployment rate.

Livingstone and others also took a strong and public stand on a series of political issues that challenged the new ideological consensus of the Tories. In particular they actively promoted measures to deal with discrimination and ran high-profile awareness campaigns against homophobia, racism and sexism. Gay and lesbian activists won funding to set up gay resource centres; poster campaigns promoted positive images of lesbians and gays on the tubes and buses; and employers and council services providers were encouraged to take positive action against discrimination. The GLC's Lesbian and Gay Charter, for example, urged that in schools, "lesbian and gay pupils and students should see reflected in the curriculum the richness and diversity of homosexual experience and not just negative images".

These activities generated a great deal of optimism and excitement on the left and among lesbian and gay activists about what could be achieved through local government.

People who had been running advice and support centres on a shoestring, in the back rooms of left wing bookshops, found they were now running committees with dedicated budgets. This reinforced the shift "out of the streets onto the committees", as one gay activist put it. In reality there were definite limits to what this strategy could achieve. As Livingstone argued after his election:

> We try to avoid people rushing away with the idea that this is going to be a revolutionary council that's going to bring down the government or transform the life in London... The manifesto is not revolutionary. If it's carried out it will be a major breakthrough, because in simple reformist terms it will be a bold step forward. It is a step that a capitalist society could live with – wouldn't like, but could live with. Most of the things in that manifesto have been done somewhere else, usually under governments which are in no sense socialist.

But the Tories wanted to smash anything that could become a focus of opposition to them. They sought to do so by cutting funding to the councils and focusing their attacks on the so-called "loony left" policies which supported gays and lesbians, women and ethnic minorities. These were seen as soft targets, which could be used to drive through a wider assault on organised workers and the left.

At the same time the Tories were waging a series of battles against different groups of workers. Having achieved a number of victories they now felt confident to take on one of the most powerful groups of organised workers in the country – the miners.

The "enemies within" strike back

Early in 1984 a programme of mass job cuts and pit closures was announced. By March a national strike was under way.

It was to continue for a year, the biggest strike in Europe's history, and proved to be a decisive battle. At one point during the dispute Thatcher told the Coal Board boss Ian MacGregor, "You have the fate of this government in your hands," and several times confided her fear that the government could lose. The Tories' victory over the miners was by no means inevitable, but it was a huge setback for the wider working class movement.

However, something else quite unexpected happened in the course of the strike that was to have a positive and lasting impact on the fight for sexual liberation.

During the strike people up and down the country debated whether they should support the miners. Huge numbers of working class people built solidarity in their trade unions, workplaces and communities. In this context Lesbians and Gays Support the Miners (LGSM) was launched in London by a small group of activists who set about promoting the miners' cause and raising money for the strike fund. Bucket collections were taken round gay bars and clubs, public meetings and gigs put on, performance poetry and plays were organised – including "Dear Love of Comrades", a reading about Edward Carpenter, and T-shirts and badges were made. Before long around ten other groups had been set up around the country.

These activities were not welcomed by all lesbians and gays. Managers at some gay venues had LGSM activists ejected for "intimidating customers" and other people raised objections: "Why support the miners? What have they done for us?" some lesbians and gays said, or, "You people should be collecting for our organisations for people with AIDS, not the miners." Those involved in the support groups came up with many inventive responses:

What do you mean the miners don't support us? The miners dig coal, which is used for fuel, which makes electricity, that runs these disco lights. Would you go down there and do it? Part of the reason I support them is they go down and do it. I wouldn't![116]

Some miners were also sceptical about any common interest between themselves and gays. Many lived in tightly knit village communities and had little experience of gays and lesbians. As one of the founders of the LGSM explains, "When the Dulais Support Group first received our letter [offering support] there were not a few raised eyebrows. Some miners were openly hostile and suggested that we would be made a laughing stock of the Valleys".[117]

The struggle changed all that. Gays and lesbians gained respect because of the solidarity they delivered, and miners who found themselves being victimised in the press and brutalised by the police began to see the need to support other groups suffering similar treatment. As Sian James, Secretary of South Wales Women Support Groups put it:

> We turned our backs on lesbians and gays, we didn't have anything to do with them, it had nothing to do with us. We might have felt sorry for them but what could you do – for years that was our attitude. But suddenly WE were up for grabs. We were being attacked by the police, the media, the state... You cannot sympathise WITH an oppressed group until you've been a member of one.[118]

This new unity forged between two unlikely groups who began to realise they faced a common enemy was powerfully expressed by a miner at a 1,500-strong "Pits and Perverts Ball" held in Camden in 1984, which raised £5,000 for the miners:

> You have worn our badge, "Coal not Dole", and you know what harassment means, as we do. Now we will pin your

badge on us, we will support you. It won't change overnight, but now 140,000 miners know that there are other causes and other problems. We know about blacks and gays and nuclear disarmament. And we will never be the same.[119]

And support gays they did. At Gay Pride in 1985 miners from Blaenant Lodge South Wales took along their banner and marched behind the official Pride banner to tunes from the Big Red brass band. That same year National Union of Mineworkers (NUM) delegates to the TUC and Labour Party conferences were central to getting official policy in support of gay rights adopted. The experience of the miners' strike boosted the commitment of many trade unionists and socialists to gay rights and also convinced some lesbian and gay activists of the importance of building alongside the working class movement. Over the next few years many more unions would commit to lesbian and gay rights and set up gay groups.

But the defeat of the miners shifted the balance of forces in society decisively in favour of the Tories. Lesbians and gays had won powerful allies in the working class, but workers' confidence to use that power had been greatly weakened. In this context the Tories were able to drive on with their agenda of cuts, privatisations and an offensive against the left, and this was to involve a major attack on lesbian and gay rights.

Throughout the miners' strike, activists had been resisting the Tories' attacks on Labour left councils' funding. Some councils declared they would defy the government's cap on rates – breaking the law – and in the middle of the miners' strike 100,000 workers had taken strike action in London. But in the wake of the miners' defeat resistance collapsed. Livingstone imposed the rate cap in London and other councils followed like dominoes. In 1986 the GLC, prized centre of many progressive activists, was abolished.

These attacks were accompanied by a sustained campaign against the "loony left" which was used by the Tories to whip up a divisive climate and smear their opposition in the run-up to the 1987 general election. Newspaper articles warned against "the paedophile aggression of loony left London boroughs", and attacked "militant perverts", "gay bullies" and "homosexual fascists". Tory MPs talked about "psychopathological perversion". Press reports that a book called *Jenny Lives with Eric and Martin* was stocked in one of London's school libraries was met with hysteria. Apparently the stories about five year old Jenny, her father Eric and his boyfriend Martin going to the launderette together, preparing a surprise birthday party and discussing why a woman had expressed homophobic disgust at them in the streets, were all too much.

Section 28 and the Tory offensive

Emboldened by winning a third election, Thatcher then used her party conference speech to complain "children are being taught they have the unalienable right to be gay".[120] This was followed up by the publication of an interview in which she claimed:

> So they are casting their problems on society and who is society? There is no such thing! There are individual men and women and there are families and no government can do anything except through people and people look to themselves first. It is our duty to look after ourselves and then also to help look after our neighbour.[121]

The Tories now went beyond rhetoric to introduce the first piece of specifically anti-gay legislation since 1885, Section 28. This banned any positive discussion of homosexuality in schools and was to contribute to a deep problem of homophobia in the education system. David Wilshire MP, who first introduced the clause, explained, "The traditional family as we know it is under attack." The new regulations stated that no local authority shall "intentionally promote homosexuality or...the acceptability of homosexuality as a pretended family relationship".

Of course the idea that homosexuality was being promoted in schools was false, since any input into the curriculum had already been taken out of the hands of local authorities. But Section 28 held great symbolic value for the Tories, who wanted to draw a very clear line between having to concede some basic civil rights to gays and lesbians and maintaining that their relationships could in no way be considered a legitimate alternative to the heterosexual family.

Trade unionists and socialists were critical to the fight against Section 28. The national teaching unions, representing tens of thousands of members, came out against it and took to the streets. The 20,000-strong march in Manchester in February 1988 was the biggest mobilisation for gay rights to have taken place in Britain, and was followed by a record 30,000 attending the annual Pride that year. But against the backdrop of a series of big defeats for our side, this was not enough to stop Section 28 passing into law.

The resistance to these attacks was consistently held back by the behaviour of the Labour Party, whose electoralism made its commitment to gay rights unreliable. From the late 1970s many activists fought hard for the issue to be taken up, but this was resisted by others who saw gay rights as a liability. The debate at Labour Party conference, which passed policy in favour of gay rights, was even scheduled to take place during the 15 minutes that the conference was not televised! In the 1983 Bermondsey by-election Labour candidate Peter Tatchell faced a vicious witch-hunt for being gay, which was whipped up by the press and opposition parties and led to numerous physical assaults on Tatchell and up to

30 death threats. After his home was attacked he slept with a fire extinguisher and a rope ladder beside his bed.[122] A Labour Party member and former Labour leader of Southwark council, John O'Grady, stood against Tatchell for "Real Bermondsey Labour". He had the backing of the former Labour MP in the area and was filmed during the campaign attacking Tatchell for wearing "his trousers back to front".

Yet the Labour Party instructed Tatchell not to answer the attacks on his sexuality and to effectively stay in the closet. In the wake of another by-election loss in 1987, this time after a candidate had been attacked for her pro-gay position, Kinnock's press secretary Patricia Hewitt wrote, "The lesbian and gay issue is costing us dear among the pensioners".[123] This was promptly leaked to the *Sun*, who used it to run a vicious anti-gay campaign in the run-up to the general election.

Activists who had looked to the Labour Party as a vehicle for change were coming up against the limitations of a reformist organisation which subordinated principles to winning elections. By 1987 the Labour leader Neil Kinnock had witch-hunted many militants out of the party and was talking about Labour offering "Thatcherism with a human face".

The left's resistance to this "long march to the right" was hamstrung by a strategy that prioritised maintaining unity in the party in order not to undermine Labour's election chances or "play into the hands" of the Tories. This was compounded by a focus on capturing positions in council and Labour Party structures which took activists away from any serious attempts to galvanise rank and file workers against the attacks they faced – even though the 100,000-strong strike in defence of the GLC had shown the potential power of such struggles. These weaknesses were reinforced by the influence of separatist and identity politics, which hardened among many women, gay and black activists in the early 1980s. The separation of questions of oppression from class suited a layer of people who, having won careers off the back of more radical struggle, were happy to make peace with the system. Patricia Hewitt, who attacked the visibility of gay rights in the Greenwich by-election, had in the early 1980s been a supporter of the left and a self-professed feminist. So while some activists from the social movements found themselves losing bitter fights to defend what had been won in the 1960s and 1970s, others were selling them out.

Those who sought to wage relatively autonomous struggles for lesbian and gay and women's rights, however, found such struggles could not ultimately withstand the larger assault taking place in British society.

AIDS

All of this was taking place at a time when lesbians and gays were to face their biggest challenge – AIDS. One of the terrible ironies about the success of the right in Britain and the US was that on most social questions, including women's and gay rights, opinion polls had shown a stable, if not strengthening, commitment to equality among the majority of the population.[124] But the moral panic generated around AIDS – dubbed the "gay plague" – threatened to turn the clock back.

AIDS had a devastating impact. It saw governments sit back and do nothing while tens of thousands of people suffered and died. Hundreds of thousands more – gay and straight – became infected, ignorant of prevention methods. The first cases were discovered in the US in 1979, but Reagan did not even mention AIDS till a speech in 1987. In Britain it was 1985 before the government earmarked resources for AIDS. In both cases this was a response to the hard campaigning of activists as the scale of risk to public health became impossible to ignore. But it was too little too late. In the US the absence of a national health service and a more severe backlash against gays meant the impact of AIDS was the most serious; by 1988 82,000 people had been diagnosed with AIDS, of whom 46,000 were already dead. Gay men of the baby-boom generation in New York suffered a 50 percent casualty rate from AIDS.[125] The sheer number of people affected meant that for many gay men AIDS was an extremely personal and relentless tragedy during which they lost lovers and friends. As if this was not hard enough the lack of legal rights for lesbians and gays meant hundreds of thousands endured the pain of lovers shut out of hospital rooms, refused involvement in important medical decisions and denied entry at funeral ceremonies – followed by losing their homes and inheritance.

The impact of AIDS was immensely disorientating. The new sexual openness of the 1970s and early 1980s was one of most prized gains of the struggle, so it was particularly cruel that tragedy should strike at "a place that had brought the deepest joy".[126] And as Charles Krauthammer pointed out, the "gay plague" came "just as homosexuality was prepared to take the last step and free itself from the medical mantle".[127] It created a crisis among activists about how to respond. At first it was not clear how HIV was spread or how it could be prevented, and some feared that dealing openly with these things would lead to severe attacks on gays.

The right took this opportunity to go on the offensive. In the US a syndicated column suggesting people with AIDS should be tattooed appeared across the nation.[128] Jerry Falwell, a key ally of Reagan, named AIDS "the judgement of God" and called for gays to be quarantined, while conservative commentator Pat Buchanan crowed, "The sexual revolution has begun to devour its children." The US government, just like the Tories, used anti-gay prejudice as a stick to beat the Democrats as "the party of quotas and gay rights". It was in this atmosphere that Reagan won a second term in 1984.

The gay writer Dennis Altman had recently said of America that "the homosexual is accepted but homosexuality is not", suggesting that while many people had been won to supporting basic human rights for gay people, they were not ready to embrace their sexuality.[129] A section of the right were now trying to prise this contradiction open, with the likes of Pat Buchanan asking, "Does the [Democratic] party maintain…its solemn commitment to federally protected civil rights for active homosexuals?"

A similar pattern emerged in Britain. James Anderton, the Chief Constable of Manchester, claimed, "People at risk are swirling around in a human cesspit of their own making".[130] A *Mail on Sunday* columnist insisted AIDS victims should be treated as "social outcasts" since "each homosexual only has his own promiscuity to blame". This came together with the mobilisation around Section 28. Even the dead were seen as fair game. The *Daily Mail*'s epitaph for celebrated actor and AIDS victim Rock Hudson was "died a living skeleton – so ashamed".

The combination of inaction and disinformation around AIDS and the backlash against gays generated huge public anxiety about the disease itself. Through the 1980s a significant number of people thought you could catch AIDS by shaking someone's hand, a situation not helped by the obscure talk of "bodily fluids" in government ads. This came with a rising homophobia. In the US a poll found those who thought homosexuality was an acceptable lifestyle dropped from 58 percent in 1982 to 51 percent in 1983.[131] In Britain 74 percent said they disapproved of gay relationships in 1987, up 12 percentage points from 1983. A massive majority, 93 percent, thought gay men should not be allowed to adopt children (83 percent for lesbians)[132] and 60 percent thought gay teachers should be sacked. Between 1986 and 1989 *Gay Times* counted 55 murders of gay men. In London the paper *Capital Gay* had its offices burned down.

In this environment a range of institutions actively encouraged discrimination against lesbians and gays. Police harassment of gays was stepped up so that in late 1980s Britain the number of convictions for consensual sex between men reached its highest since records began.[133] The Conservative Family Campaign produced a "Charter of Responsibility for HIV Sufferers" which called for them to be banned from some occupations including food processing.[134] Author and activist Jeffrey Weeks reports that "ambulance drivers disinfected their vehicles, prison officers refused to deal with people with AIDS, policemen wore gloves and protective clothing while raiding gay bars, theatre personnel refused to work with gay actors, children with the virus were banned from schools, the press sought to expose famous and not so famous people if they were suspected of having AIDS".[135] In the gay heartland of San Francisco the municipal government issued masks and gloves to firefighters and police officers for use in their dealings with homosexuals during emergency work.

The immense stupidity and bigotry with which our ruling classes responded to AIDS, and their ongoing refusal to pump the proper resources into finding a cure and caring for the sick, has caused millions of people around the world to pay with their lives, and those of friends and loved ones. When the first laying of the AIDS memorial quilt took place in Washington in 1987 it was bigger than a football pitch with each 3 foot by 6 panel representing a human grave; now it is so large that there is no public space in the US where it could be laid out in full.

Yet faced with debilitating illnesses, death and a huge anti-gay backlash, people with HIV and AIDS formed the backbone of a militant fightback. Where the state refused to provide support, they set up organisations and services which gave advice and practical help to those with HIV/AIDS and their relatives. While governments and the media persisted in mystifying AIDS, activists pioneered safe sex practices.

This resistance brought a new generation of people into activity and organisation, especially in the US where the crisis was more acute. The AIDS Coalition to Unleash Power (ACT UP), for example, had 40 branches around the US at its height and its "Silence=Death" posters and pink triangle logo regularly covered major cities. ACT UP's meetings and activities involved hundreds, sometimes thousands, of people. They sat-in at pharmaceutical company Burroughs Wellcome's HQ calling for prices of AIDS drugs to be dropped, chained themselves to the New York Stock Exchange urging them to unload shares in this company, marched to the White House demanding money for research instead of war, occupied the Food and Drug Administration (FDA) to call for research and picketed the anti-gay press. These struggles won small but invaluable victories. The FDA was forced to speed up drugs testing, prices went down and placebos were largely taken off trials.

Turning the tide on the backlash

For a time in the late 1980s it appeared as if the bigots had successfully turned the clocks back on lesbian and gay rights, but by the 1990s it was apparent that the reversals were temporary and the general situation for most people continued to improve. This was reflected in a whole number of measures from legislation to the increased visibility and participation of lesbians and gays at every level in society. A poll conducted in the US in 1985 found that only 25 percent of Americans had friends, relatives or colleagues who were out; by 2000 that number had tripled to 75 percent.

Central to understanding the enduring gains of lesbians and gays through this period is the resistance that they, alongside others, put up every time an attack was waged. The atmosphere of rising homophobia and desperate situation facing people with AIDS had the effect of pushing activists – lesbian, gay, bisexual, trans and straight – together in struggle. One very positive effect of this was to undermine some of the separatist politics that reigned in the early to mid 1980s. The increasingly common use of LGBT as a term reflected this inclusivity.

In the US thousands of people came out time and again to fight the attacks on lesbians and gays – sometimes with the energy and verve of the 1960s. In 1977 tens of thousands demonstrated across several states when the singer Anita Bryant succeeded in her "Save Our Children" initiative overturning Florida's municipal ban on sexual orientation discrimination. The following year lesbian and gay activists joined with trade unionists to stop John Briggs's Proposition 6, which would have banned gays from certain jobs in California. Only weeks later Harvey Milk, a leading figure in the Stop Briggs Campaign and one of the first out gay people elected to public office, was shot dead by his former colleague Dan White. Milk had been an inspiration to millions of lesbians and gays, and when a minimum sentence was handed down to his murderer it provoked a night of rioting in San Francisco so large and angry that it became known as the "White night riots". Into the 1980s and 1990s resistance continued from the courageous fightback against AIDS to the million-strong march on Washington in 1993.

In Britain a series of struggles were waged against the Tory attacks, which although they often ended in defeat, helped to create a powerful constituency of support for LGBT rights among the organised working class. Section 28 may have passed into law, but no prosecution was ever brought. This is partly because many teachers ended up policing themselves, but it also suggests the Tories were nervous about testing the organised opposition of trade unionists to this policy. There were, for example, many instances where teachers found creative ways of "breaking the law". At my college one lecturer ran a sociology class centred on the injustice faced by gay people. Since he spent the session promoting gay rights he asked the class to vote on who would support him if he was prosecuted under Section 28. He then concluded the lesson by writing the words "disease and death" on the board and claiming that the government has said this is the context that makes our discussion about gays legal.

The experience of the miners' strike and campaign against Section 28 were significant in that they involved a layer of LGBT, left and working class activists putting into practice the socialist approach to sexual politics that had been so distorted and lost in the decades preceding Stonewall. However, the fruits of those struggles were very contradictory. Activists found they were able to generate widening support for LGBT rights but they were often waging defensive campaigns focused on fighting off attacks. In this context the agenda pursued by many LGBT activists continued on a trajectory that took them away from the politics of liberation and set their sights on reform and equal rights. This approach was institutionalised in the organisations that developed.

The most notable of these organisations in Britain was the Stonewall Group (later known as Stonewall), which was launched in the wake of Section 28. They "set out to...prevent such attacks on lesbians, gay men and bisexuals from ever occurring again"[136] and placed the goal of full legal equality for LGB people at the centre of their strategy. Over the following decade Stonewall was to make an important contribution towards achieving this aim, helping to win new legal rights that have contributed to a dramatically improved situation for LGB people.

However, their success in winning legal change has also posed once again the question of how we fight the deep rooted and ongoing oppression of LGBT people in our society despite the achievement of formal equality. It is important to understand that the key factor making legal change possible in recent years has been the legacy of the big grassroots battles waged in the 1970s and 1980s, and the confidence this gave individuals to come out. These were fundamental in shaping a climate more favourable to LGBT rights and putting the social weight of organised workers behind them. Reformers in the 1990s and beyond have found themselves pushing at an open door.

Yet Stonewall was launched because its founders felt street politics had failed in the fight to stop Section 28. Instead they set out to build "a professional lobbying group"[137] centred on influencing government and mainstream political parties by employing a team of lobbyists with the backing of prominent individuals and powerful institutions. This approach was reflected in the composition of Stonewall's founders: actor Sir Ian McKellen, former Tory MP and journalist Matthew Parris, actor Michael Cashman and activist Lisa Power. It has involved focusing in on a very limited agenda that can have appeal across the political spectrum: winning legal reform and pressing employers and institutions to implement equal opportunities and good practice.

This work is important, but it also involves a pressure towards respectability. One important reflection of this is Stonewall's refusal to include trans people in their agenda – even though there are very close links between transphobia and homophobia in society at large and trans people are a group that has seen the slowest improvements in their situation. It also implies a reliance on those in power to support us. Currently Stonewall receives 26 percent of its funding from government agencies, 19 percent from corporate donations and 35 percent from individuals.[138] But what happens if the generally favourable climate towards LGBT rights changes and with it the willingness of those in positions of power to support reforms?

In the US the recent attack on gay marriage in California is a reminder of how fragile our legal rights are. The campaign to defend it was criticised by some activists for relying too much on Democratic Party support to win – even though US president Barack Obama made clear his personal discomfort with gay marriage. This meant those leading the campaign avoided making a strong case for gay marriage even though the attack asserted "only marriage between a man and a woman is valid or recognised in California", and failed to galvanise the huge numbers of people who were later to pour onto the streets after Proposition 8 was passed.

We could face a similar problem here. The difficulty with a professional lobby group is it lacks both the roots and political orientation to galvanise a movement. The question of how best to defend our rights is important. But we also have to go beyond a political consensus which centres on formal equality in favour of a transformative approach to sexual politics. If we are out for liberation, a more radical agenda will be required.

In search of a new radicalism

One reaction to the narrowing horizons of LGBT politics in the early 1990s was the launch of Queer Nation in the US and Outrage! in Britain. Initiated by former members of ACT UP, Queer Nation set out to build militant opposition to a government which had contributed to the AIDS crisis and to provide an alternative to the civil rights agenda of other LGBT organisations and the commercial gay scene, both of which were seen as compliant with the establishment. They mobilised direct action and civil disobedience against manifestations of "heterosexism" and organised celebrations of "queer culture" and the "queer nation". Chapters were set up in a number of major cities and some of the mobilisations organised by them were very big. These included marches against gay bashing, involvement in demonstrations supporting abortion rights, and sit-ins and pickets against Cracker Barrel chain after it sacked lesbian and gay employees for contravening "American family values".

However, by 1994 Queer Nation had foundered on a set of politics which very quickly fostered division. The identification of heterosexism as the enemy, for example, failed to address how LGBT oppression is anchored in a wider system of oppression and exploitation. Inevitably straight society and straight people were identified as the problem. New York's Queer Nation founding manifesto declared "We hate straights" and carried with it a visceral moralism towards those who did not experience homophobia themselves:

> Go tell straights to go away until they have spent a month walking hand in hand in public with someone of the same sex. After they survive that, then you'll hear what they have to say about queer anger. Otherwise tell them to shut up and listen.[139]

These statements reflected an angry bitterness felt by activists in America at a time when tens of thousands were dying from AIDS, but resulted in a dismissal of the prospects of winning allies in the fight against oppression. This was indicated by the use of the term "queer" itself, which activists sought to reclaim simply by wearing it as a badge of pride. As one activist put it, "We have disempowered them by using this term".[140] The problem was that a few hundred activists could not undo the weight of prejudice attached to a word which remains one of the worst terms of abuse used against lesbians and especially gay men. In the 1960s the movement had ditched "homosexual", "queer" and other words for "gay and proud" and "gay is good" in the process of battling against the ideas and institutions that oppressed them. In contrast "queer" was chosen as an assertion against a hostile world: "We're the people straight society loves to hate," as *Queer Nation* put it, and, "When a lot of lesbians and gay men wake up in the morning we feel angry and disgusted, not gay... Using queer is a way of reminding us how we are perceived by the rest of the world".[141]

A series of struggles through the 1980s had shown how straight people could be won to understanding the oppression of LGBT people and a common struggle against it – without having to experience it themselves. Remember the miner who said, "You have worn our badge... Now we will pin your badge on us." But Queer Nation's attack on straights as the problem and the use of language which many progressive activists in the wider movement rejected, cut off the potential for these kinds of reciprocal struggles.

The idea that straight society was the problem also reinforced the influence of lifestyle politics among some activists, for whom being or acting queer was seen as a political challenge to oppression in itself. As one Queer Nation flyer put it, "You as an alive and functioning queer are revolutionary".[142] But individual lifestyles do not have the power to uproot the institutions that systematically oppress us, and the rise of the "pink pound" has shown that even capitalism can find ways of making money out of different sexual identities. One Outrage! event included a celebration of Soho's gay bars and clubs on Valentine's Day – an illustration of how radical individualism can easily slide into less than radical politics of consumer power.

This emphasis on personal politics was accompanied by an extreme moralism towards lesbians and gays in the closet who were urged to come out to bear witness to the pain of oppression, and a campaign to out high-profile lesbians and gays. The thinking behind this was that celebrities and politicians should not be allowed to be complicit in the suffering of gays through their silence. But it created an atmosphere in which outing came to be seen as threatening individuals with a dirty secret, rather than a choice that can represent a step towards greater personal freedom and gay pride. By creating scandal around gay people's sexuality it undoubtedly made it harder for many people to come out in their family, workplace and community.

Although queer politics originated in the struggles of the late 1980s, it was given intellectual weight by the theories of postmodernism and post-structuralism circulating in academia at the time. These were developed by a generation of intellectuals seeking to come to terms with the failure of 1968 to achieve social transformation, and claimed to offer a new alternative to Marxism. They rejected materialism in favour of examining how discourse, ideology and culture shape the world – and dismissed the working class as a potential force for change. As one queer theorist put it:

> We are now in a period of decline and discouragement. We have no objective guarantee that the working class recognises capitalism as the cause of injustice and inequalities of American life. The recent history of the American working class clearly shows that it lacks the organisational and political capacity to struggle effectively for the fundamental transformation of society.[143]

Queer theory, which developed in the early 1990s, was shaped by such ideas but it was also a reaction to radical feminism and identity politics and, like queer activism, sought to forge a more radical set of ideas for the movement. The American academic and activist Judith Butler, for example, was very critical of the way in which feminism and patriarchy theory accepts the idea that there are inherent divisions between men and women when really gender and gender divisions are socially constructed. She also challenged the notion women can speak with the same voice regardless of "colour, sexuality, ethnicity, class and ablebodiness".

A shared concern in queer theory was the partial incorporation of the LGBT movement which failed to challenge the overall structures of sexual or gender oppression, either by appealing for rights on the basis that we are "just the same" or signing up to a set of identity labels – L, G, B or T – which accept that "we" are different from the "norm". In place of both an integrationist, civil rights approach and "exclusionary" identity politics "queer" was intended to be an inclusive home for all those who reject traditional gender identities and distinct sexual identities such as gay, lesbian and straight. As Butler put it:

> Queer is a term that desires that you don't have to present an identity card before entering a meeting. Heterosexuals can join the queer movement. Bisexuals can join the queer movement. Queer is not being lesbian. Queer is not being gay. It is an argument against lesbian specificity: that if I am a lesbian I have to desire in a certain way. Or if I am a gay I have to desire in a certain way. Queer is an argument against certain normativity, what a proper lesbian or gay identity is.[144]

Queer theory represented a step forward from some of the ideas held by lesbian and gay activists in the 1980s, in particular its rejection of separatism, which had proved to be so divisive, and a challenge to the notion that gender and sexuality is a natural given. Its search for a transgressive politics which could imagine a world beyond that which currently exists is also important. It is perhaps for these reasons that queer theory has continued to grow in stature and popularity on university campuses, especially among those seeking an alternative to the narrowed horizons of LGBT politics that has come to dominate since the decline of the gay liberation movement.

However, there are many ways in which queer theory is unable to answer how we achieve this project of creating a radical rupture with the status quo. There is, for example, an (intentional) refusal to locate the material roots of gender and sex "constructions" that contribute to our oppression. Instead a multiplicity of sources is found in "the juridical structures of language and politics" which "constitute the contemporary field of power".[145] But this creates a theoretical cul-de-sac in which the question of what is shaping these structures and how we transform them is unanswered and leads to an emphasis on the need for individual and personal resistance to oppression. So Butler argues it is through our "refusal to identify" that we "denaturalise everyday practices" and celebrates drag for its "subversive intent".

But this takes us back toward precisely the identity politics which queer theory seeks to escape, and is unable to take us beyond partial, fleeting challenges to the system. For Marxists the way out of this conundrum lies in a theory of class. This is key to understanding the material roots of oppression and locating where the power lies to overthrow it. In this framework what's transgressive is action by the working class to change the world.

Finally there remains a problem with the notion that "queer" can simply be reclaimed for progressive politics. The language we use must surely flow from the kind of struggles we are seeking to wage. "LGBT" as a label may fail to capture the unlimited rainbow of sexualities and gender identity that are possible in human society, but it is a political term that has emerged out of the struggle against oppression. This means that most people standing up to discrimination in their community or place of work see it as a step forward from the many abusive terms and labels that continue to be thrown at LGBT people. "Queer", on the other hand, remains for the vast majority of people a cruel term of abuse which most activists strongly reject.

If we want to develop a language that more truly reflects human sexuality, it will have to be connected to a far-reaching struggle for the liberation of sexuality. During the 1960s and 1970s, for example, the word "gay" had quite wide associations linked to ideas of sexual freedom – anyone could join in and sing Tom Robinson's "Glad to Be Gay". Similarly "black" was widely used as a political term of resistance by many non-white people. As those struggles waned, the wider political association of such terms also receded and became more about personal not political identity.

So how do we begin to shape a radical politics that is able to link the fight for sexual freedom to a renewed struggle to transform the world? In order to determine this we need to understand the situation we are in today.

LGBT Pride march, London, 2000
© Jess Hurd www.reportdigital.co.uk

6: The way we are now – is this as good as it gets?

By the early 1990s the Tory government had achieved its central objective of beating key sections of the organised working class. But in the process it had generated massive discontent. A series of bitter social protests from the poll tax riots that finally ended Thatcher's reign, to the near general strike against the pit closures in 1992, shook the government profoundly.

The Tories' appeal to ultra-conservative family values also no longer had any credibility. John Major's "Back to Basics" campaign sank in a quagmire of Tory sleaze and double standards. Meanwhile working class resistance to their attacks from the year-long miners' strike to the campaign against Section 28 had contributed to winning a more generally accepted consensus in favour of LGBT rights. This was something that even the Tories had to recognise when they reduced the age of consent for gay men from 21 to 18 in 1994.

These shifts culminated in New Labour's landslide victory in 1997 which was welcomed with relief and hope by many activists. Among the election highlights was the defeat of Michael Portillo, one of the most rabid government ministers, who lost his seat to openly gay candidate Stephen Twigg.

But Labour also came to power having accepted much of the economic agenda of the rich and powerful who had wanted the working class defeated in order to increase levels of exploitation. As Peter Mandelson put it, "New Labour's mission is to move forward from where Margaret Thatcher left off, rather than dismantle every single thing she did".[146]

Labour's pursuit of these economic policies involved a

sustained attack on the very people who had supported it and generated considerable discontent. In a bid to shore up its support Labour reached for some of the same old scapegoats and ideas, including family values.

In this way a government that was to introduce a raft of legislation in support of LGBT rights was also to cause a series of problems for those fighting for sexual liberation.

The world we have won

The gains that have been made for LGBT rights in Britain over the last two decades have been so significant that it appears not a single area of life has escaped the struggle for change. Gay priests celebrate civil ceremonies, the British Army's magazine *Soldier* features a gay trooper on its cover next to the headline "Pride" and Tory prime minister David Cameron predicts the first gay prime minister will be a Conservative one.

A recent poll found that up to 90 percent of people back laws banning discrimination against gays while 73 percent think such discrimination calls for corrective action.[147]

One of the most important areas of change has been the legal reforms which have removed some of the most bigoted anti-gay laws and introduced basic human rights previously denied to LGBT people. These include the scrapping of Section 28 and an end to the ban on gays in the military; the legal right to challenge homophobia at work and discrimination in other areas of life; legal recognition for transsexuals; and the introduction of civil partnerships.

All of these have had a positive impact that should not be underestimated. Civil partnerships finally ended the injustice and heartbreak endured by millions of couples denied "next of kin" status. This had not only deprived us of benefits, pension and inheritance rights but also the right to be at our partner's hospital bedside in times of sickness, or even to be contacted in the event of their death. They have brought a recognition of gay relationships that has been systematically denied by the establishment for over a century. As one pensioner couple, Roger (77) and Percy (66), put it:

After 40 years of being together...our love does not need proclaiming as such, but there is...importance in making our fellow citizens aware that there are other people with other lifestyles in the universe. As I have got older I have got much more militant, this is a political as well as an emotional statement.[148]

This social change has been achieved by our struggles, big and small, collective and individual, over the last few decades. These have created a powerful constituency in society that makes it difficult for those in power to ever again dismiss gay rights as simply a "minority" interest. The struggle against Section 28 did not succeed, but its mobilisation of the organised trade union movement helped to shape a climate which saw John Major inviting gay actor Ian McKellen into Downing Street during a campaign for the age of consent for gay men to be equalised. Since then almost every trade union has developed an LGBT group and has incorporated LGBT rights into its agenda. With a combined membership of over six million people, developments in these unions played a major role in shifting public opinion generally and putting pressure on Labour to deliver change.

The improvement in women's rights and the changing shape of the modern family have also helped to create a more positive situation for LGBT rights.

In just a few generations there has been increasing diversity in the way people choose to live their relationships, conduct their sex lives and bring up children. This has weakened the traditional family and changed the values people hold on to when deciding how they live their lives. As Jeffrey

Weeks has pointed out:

> Thatcher was welcomed by moral conservatives as the champion of traditional values...who would halt and push back the tide of social and moral change. Yet during the decade or more of her period in office, and continuing under her successor, all the indices show an acceleration of change.[149]

In 2007, for example, the number of couples getting married, at just 236,000, was the lowest since records began in 1885 – a 31 percent drop since 1991.[150] Alongside this has been an increase in the number of people cohabiting or living single and a rise in the number of children born outside of marriage and those living in one-parent families. The Office for National Statistics, which compiles all this data, anticipates many of these trends will continue or accelerate. A recent report estimated that by 2031 the number of cohabiting couples will have increased by two thirds from today.[151]

Underlying these headline statistics is the continued impact of the structural changes and social upheavals that took place in capitalism after the Second World War: the expansion of higher education and massive influx of women into work; advances in terms of people's intimate relationships from divorce laws to abortion rights and the pill; and the struggles waged by mass movements and trade unionists which shaped the impact and outcome of these changes.

The changed expectations of women today are particularly striking in comparison even to their grandmothers' times. Whereas in the past many women's prospects were tied to their roles as wives and mothers, there are now increasing numbers of women who may never marry or have children. Pregnancy and sex outside of marriage could once bring shame, ostracism and even detention under the Mental Health Act.[152] But women today are far more confident about expressing their sexuality and satisfying their sexual needs.

This is part of a much wider shift in people's sex lives, which have become increasingly separated from questions of marriage and reproduction.

As a consequence, people's attitudes towards different kinds of relationships are much less restricted by a set of conventions tied to the family. This has made it easier for LGBT people to make relationships of their choosing and to be open about them. The advent of civil partnerships, which has seen almost 27,000 couples tie the knot since its inception in December 2005,[153] has undoubtedly contributed to this, giving many same-sex couples an opportunity to share their relationship with family, friends and workmates.

The more open and public activity of LGBT people has also generated a sizeable economy which can act as an incentive for even sections of business and the establishment to support certain LGBT rights. In early 1990s Birmingham, for example, there was one gay club; now there is a gay quarter, cheek by jowl with the Chinese quarter. This process has been repeated across many major cities including London, Manchester, Leeds, Liverpool, Brighton, Margate, Bournemouth and Blackpool. Alongside the scene, a plethora of "gay" products, "gay" identities and "gay" activities have appeared on the market, from alcohol to tourism and honeymoons, such that a 2006 survey estimated the pink economy in Britain to be worth £70 billion.[154]

With the growing market, it has become good business sense to encourage a safe climate in which LGBT people can "consume" their products free from fear and harassment. Developing a gay-friendly portfolio has also come to be seen as a means of both cornering the gay market and attracting gay talent and skills into business. The *Fortune* survey of the top 500 US companies revealed that 80 percent of them had anti-discriminatory policies and saw them as "good for business".[155] This has created a situation in which some sections of the establishment oppose LGBT rights while others support them. In the US, for example, Google came out against the successful Proposition 8 campaign to ban gay marriage in California.

New Labour – the great reforming government?

The role of New Labour in delivering the gains currently enjoyed by LGBT people needs to be assessed in the context of these social changes. During their time in government we saw a century of anti-gay laws swept away and now have some of the best legislation in the world on LGBT rights. This has led some activists to see a Labour government as the best means of achieving full equality, with Jeffrey Weeks referring to Labour as a "great reforming government" helping to complete the "long unfinished sexual revolution".

There is no question that Labour's approach in government was a world apart from the days of Thatcher and the Tories, who some fear will revive a crude anti-gay agenda now they are back in office. In part this was a response to the general shift in public opinion in favour of LGBT rights, which other parties have also had to reflect. Labour's support also lies among a layer of activists and trade unionists who pushed for improved rights, and organisations like Stonewall have systematically lobbied Labour to bring LGB equality into law. The most recent figures suggesting LGBT people make up 6 percent of the population has also made the "pink vote" important.

But the Labour government generally followed the call for reform, rather than leading it. One of the slogans when Labour was elected in 1997 was "Tony Blair, we won't wait, scrap Section 28!" yet it was only repealed in 2003, and other key reforms were not introduced until Labour's second and third term. When they were introduced they were not delivered in a systematic and principled way. The equalising of the age of consent, the lifting of the ban on gays in the military, and the outlawing of discrimination against gays at work were all initiated following directives from the European courts – the last of them having initially been opposed by Labour. Much of the legislation including lowering the age of consent and repealing Section 28 was also treated as "free votes" in parliament – as if LGBT rights are a matter of moral conscience rather than principle.

In a number of areas there remains a double standard for LGBT people – civil partnerships still deny us the right to marry – a form of segregation which would rightly cause outrage if applied to any other group in society. Trans people who wish to apply for a gender recognition certificate must get a divorce if they are married.

Labour also failed to use its position in government to follow through on legislation by taking action against homophobia and transphobia.

One of the areas that seems to run counter to the shift in favour of LGBT people is schools. Stonewall's *The School Report* found almost two thirds of young lesbian, gay and bisexual people had suffered homophobic bullying at school. Yet many schools are reluctant to do anything about it. Only a quarter of schools across the UK openly condemn homophobic bullying even though where they do LGBT students are 60 percent less likely to be bullied. When a straight teacher approached her head to suggest the school take steps to tackle homophobia she was told, "Our school is not ready for that kind of thing." Sixty percent of young LGBT people asked said they felt there was not a single adult they could come out to. No wonder the report found that many young LGBT people try to kill themselves rather than come out.[156]

Action on this is particularly urgent given the recent survey showing that one in four attacks against LGBT people are committed by 16 to 20 year olds.[157] The murder of David Morley, a man who had survived the Soho nail bombing only to be killed in 2004 while strolling along the Southbank, and the killing of Michael Causer, who was dragged from a house party in 2008 where he had fallen asleep, and then abused and battered before being dumped on the street, were committed by young people.

The horrific effects of homophobic and transphobic attacks and murders are not confined to their victims or relatives. Every LGBT person lives in fear that prejudice or hostility could slide into something more dangerous.

But it would be wrong to think the only problem facing LGBT people is a few homophobic thugs. According to the Gay British Crime Survey 2008, only 1 percent of victims of homophobic hate crime reported that someone had been convicted of the offence.[158] This figure suggests an institutionalised homophobia and transphobia in the justice system and wider society similar to the institutionalised racism uncovered by the Stephen Lawrence inquiry.

A recent employment survey found that one in five lesbians and gays had experienced homophobic bullying in the last five years.[159] This followed the TUC's report that showed 44 percent of 450 LGB trade unionists asked had suffered discrimination ranging from harassment to being sacked. Incidents included an office worker who had a noose left on his desk and a firefighter who was subjected to a series of abusive phone calls in which he was accused of having AIDS.[160]

Television presenters like Graham Norton and TV shows such as *The L Word* suggest we have come a long way since the first gay kiss on British television in *EastEnders* in 1987 saw it dubbed "Eastbenders" by the tabloid press for showing such "filth". Yet in 2006 of 196 prime time hours viewed on BBC1 and BBC2 lesbians and gays were presented positively for just six minutes.[161] In over half of the coverage lesbians and gays were the focus of jokes. When people complained following Chris Moyles's use of the word "gay" to describe a "rubbish" ring tone in front of six million listeners, the BBC took no action. After a *Daily Mail* article by Jan Moir implying the death of gay singer Stephen Gately was the result of an unnatural lifestyle the Press Complaints Commission (PCC) received over 25,000 complaints – a record – including one lodged by Gately's civil partner. Yet the PCC claimed it was not possible to identify "any prejudicial language in the article". This contrasts with the furore over the Jonathan Ross/Russell Brand "Sachsgate" in 2008, in which prank telephone calls and lewd answerphone messages resulted in suspensions, resignations and even condemnation from the prime minister.

Much has been made of the number of senior politicians in recent times who have openly admitted to being gay. However, there was only one out lesbian in parliament under Labour and Gordon Brown turned down his invitation to attend Pride 2009 due to "security", sending Sarah Brown, his wife, instead.

So there remains in Britain a huge gap between the formal rights that have been won and the brute reality of oppression and discrimination still experienced by many LGBT people.

While new laws are in place, old laws continue to be mobilised against consenting adults engaged in same-sex activity. In 2008 a 70 year old man was arrested and charged with cottaging. He hanged himself before the case could go to trial. I wonder if he felt, after all these years and all the change he must have seen, whether we had indeed "arrived"?

Today it is very common to talk about the LGBT community as if we are all one big happy family. But the reality is there are real divisions, not just of experience but also of politics and class interest. Of course no one can escape oppression just because of their wealth or class. Justin Fashanu, who hanged himself after constant hounding following his coming out, was the first £1 million black footballer. This is an appalling reminder that oppression has to be challenged in every walk of life.

But money generally does bring with it choices, a lifestyle and resources that make the chances of avoiding or limiting the experience of homophobia much greater. A major problem facing young LGBT people when they are rejected by their families is homelessness – in contrast with the gay Labour MP Chris Bryant, who reportedly "double flipped" his home after "lewd graffiti" appeared on his constituency home, making a £77,000 profit in the process.

The Way We Are Now, edited by the chief executive of Stonewall, Ben Summerskill, gives a snapshot of the lives of lesbians and gays in the 21st century as seen through the eyes of various middle class professionals: writers, consultants, journalists, a police commissioner, a concert pianist, a chief director and one trade unionist. Most of them talk about their experiences of homophobia, but this mainly relates to the issue of coming out and there is a consensus that discrimination is a thing of the past. Matthew Parris, for example, ends his piece by suggesting "we should stop thinking of ourselves as special…self-pity is the final closet and others' sympathies our final chains".[162]

This picture is far removed from the challenges faced by many LGBT people on the way to work, at work, in school, at home, on the street. It is not simply that class shapes our experience of oppression, but it is fundamental to the bread and butter issues shaping our daily lives – housing, health, education and work. And yet the politics that has come to prevail is one that treats gay politics as if it is a single-issue question. This in itself is a form of class politics which best fits those privileged enough to be able to worry only about the barriers presented to them because of their sexuality or gender identity in separation from everything else.

But it has also helped to facilitate attempts by those in positions of power to seize the LGBT agenda for their own ends. Thus we had the spectacle of both the Tories and Labour in the run-up to the 2010 election rowing over who deserves the "pink vote" – a row seemingly suspended from their wider policies which have both been a disaster for millions of people.

In New Labour's Britain LGBT rights were integrated into a set of ideas that reflected the interests and values of market capitalism. Every individual was to be assisted to become a citizen through a set of formal rights without any real challenge to institutional oppression. Human rights rhetoric was even mobilised in support of imperialist wars, as happened with the use of women's rights and gay rights to justify the occupation and invasion of the Middle East, wars which have killed millions and contributed to the persecution of oppressed groups.

Selling us our rights

The redefinition of gays and lesbians as citizen-consumers has been encouraged by the growth of the pink economy. The expansion of social space and the greater openness around gay sexuality is a major step forward for LGBT people that we must defend. But it is also shaped and distorted by the needs of big business and the market, with everything from choosing a look to looking for sex distorted by money and market transactions.

In theory the pink economy offers a dazzling choice of lifestyles, identities and experiences for people with different shapes, sizes and needs catered for. But in reality it plays a major role in promoting a very narrow set of ideas and values all geared towards getting us to spend money. The gay identity we are sold is generally skinny, wears designer clothes, is in search of sexual gratification and is ironically stereotypically gendered. So the trendy gay male is supposed to look boyish, toned, hairless and tanned. Little wonder then that plastic surgery and eating disorders are both more prevalent among gay men compared to their straight peers, and on the rise.

There has also been the rise of "raunch culture" in the LGBT scene, which now abounds with opportunities to buy and consume sex from strip nights to free porn sheets, chat lines, rent boys and the rest. It is not surprising there should be a growing market for these things in a society that continually undermines opportunities for genuine sexual expression, particularly for LGBT people. But what is particularly galling about this development is the way it is sold to us as something empowering, when it often involves degrading forms of work and human relationships.

In place of collective liberation, the market has intervened to offer a form of individual empowerment which has no limits but your spending power, a philosophy which mirrors the rapacious individualism of capitalism.

This is most poignantly illustrated in what has happened to Pride. This once militant commemoration of the Stonewall riots has been replaced with a corporate-sponsored day out. The theme for London Pride 2009, held just months after the election of two Nazi BNP members to the European parliament, was simply "Come Out and Play". One million people attended, including an unprecedented number of trade union delegations and huge numbers of young people, and there was a great deal of criticism of the depoliticisation of Pride. When asked about this, one of its organisers, Paul Birrell, answered:

> If we were heavily politicised, there's no way we would be in Oxford Street and Regent Street. The traders wouldn't want it and they have a lot of clout with the council, but when they can see it attracts people into the city, they're happy.[163]

So we have won important gains, but these gains are consistently threatened, limited, distorted and incorporated by a capitalist system that continues to rest on inequality and oppression.

Neoliberalism, family values and scapegoats

The neoliberal policies pursued by all parties over the last three decades have intensified this inequality. Central to this has been the drive to raise the profitability and competitiveness of British capitalism by cheapening labour costs, cutting and privatising public services and reducing regulations on finance and big business. Work has become unbearable for larger numbers of workers subject to long hours, shift work, targets, short-term contracts and surveillance. The combination of cuts, privatisation and marketisation in our public services and welfare has put pressure on individuals to shoulder the burden and costs of once common services. So the sell-off of council housing has left councils unable to provide social housing while low benefit levels condemn the unemployed to abject poverty. Meanwhile deregulation has increased the profits of major corporations and financial institutions while they gamble with our savings and pensions.

These attacks have generated a mass of social problems from homelessness to student debt and historic levels of inequality which should all be laid at the feet of government. It is in seeking to avoid this outcome that Labour in power reached for the old scapegoats and "family values".

One consequence of these attacks has been a growing pressure on the family to provide support and resources previously provided by the state. Faced with the evidence that there are only seven day nursery places for every 100 children under eight in Britain, Labour ministers suggested that grandparents should step in. Overall it is estimated that 93 percent of childcare costs are now borne by the family. Meanwhile the cuts in student grants and introduction of fees have seen a massive rise in the number of young people living at home well into their twenties.

The importance of the family in providing essential services and childcare on the cheap shaped the Labour government's social and moral agenda around the family which it mobilised both as a means of "Bringing Britain together" and stigmatising those who don't fit in. A key element of this has been eulogising "working families'" as the cornerstone of a "decent society".

This has been accompanied by a poorhouse morality which blames failing families for all manner of social problems from "hoodies" and gun and knife crime to poverty and poor housing – in a language which bears striking similarity to the Victorian notion of the "deserving" and "undeserving poor". Thus Brown gave tax credits to low-paid working families while forcing single parents to work for benefits. This punishment of working class communities has informed a social authoritarianism which reached parts even the Tories had feared to tread in the 1980s. Young people have been criminalised with ASBOs and curfews and parents shunted into parenting classes and even jail for their children's behaviour. These are now major themes peddled in Cameron's talk of "broken Britain" which focuses on all the social ills supposedly caused by the broken family.

Such an approach has also served to stigmatise those whose lifestyles or relationships in any way challenge the traditional family. As Jack Straw put it:

> The absence of prejudice should not mean the absence of rules, order or stability… Let our social morality be based on reason…not bigotry. But let us not delude ourselves that we can build a society fit for our children to grow up in without making a moral judgement about the nature of that society… Any decent society is founded on duty and responsibility.

It is this reliance on the family, on "making a moral judgement" about the kinds of "rules" people should live by at a time when a growing number of people support LGBT rights, that explains Labour's tightrope walking in relation to LGBT rights. For a section of the establishment civil partnerships offered a way not only of responding to pressure for change, but of doing so in a way that protected the family institution. So Labour abandoned Ron Davies after his visit to Clapham Common (an area where people go to look for gay sex) was exposed in the press, suspending and investigating him for "bringing the party into disrepute". Another Labour MP, Gordon McMaster, committed suicide after a "whispering campaign" about his sexual orientation. For New Labour one expression of sexuality is acceptable – the other isn't.

Of course civil partnerships should be defended, but they should also be recognised as being partly about maintaining people's commitment to, and illusions in, the family. Yet the family continues to be the root of the problem of LGBT oppression and can be place which is full of horror, whether it's a violent reaction to a family member coming out, domestic violence or child abuse.

So the gains we have won remain precarious, unstable and under threat. It is a situation fundamentally shaped by the policies and interests of those in power; one where the reactionary *Sun* newspaper can celebrate Elton John's civil partnership but David Morley can be beaten to death on the Southbank.

These murders are a tragic reminder that we not riding on an arc of inevitable progress where the main battles we face are to overcome outdated prejudice rooted in the past. Rather the system renews our oppression on a daily basis; and it also creates a situation in which the things we win can also be pushed back.

Demonstration against Section 28, April 1988
© Andrew Wilard

7: A world to win

On the evening of 30 October 2009 around 8,000 people held a vigil in Trafalgar Square, London, where weeks earlier Ian Baynham, a gay man, had been battered to death by teenagers. This was no backstreet, but the heart of London, a city traditionally considered the safest in which to come out – and just a five-minute walk from the gay area in Soho. In the same month BNP leader Nick Griffin used his appearance on the BBC's flagship programme *Question Time* to say he found the sight of two men kissing "creepy". Just days later James Parkes was beaten to within an inch of his life in Liverpool by over a dozen people as he left a gay bar. A series of statistics for the year showed a significant increase in reported homophobic attacks in London (20 percent) and Liverpool (40 percent) as well as in Glasgow (32 percent) and Greater Manchester (63 percent).[164]

The response to these events was big and angry. Several thousand surrounded the BBC to try and stop Griffin, clashing repeatedly with police, and ensuring that our protests against a Nazi on primetime TV dominated the media for the next 24 hours. Vigils involving several hundred to 2,000 people were held around the country in protest at the killing of Ian Baynham and the spate of homophobic attacks. In Liverpool over 2,000 people, gay and straight, young and old, some wielding their union banners, joined a spirited demonstration against homophobic attacks, led by the mother of Michael Causer, the victim of a fatal homophobic attack.

These protests sent a strong message to the bigots that there would be no turning back, no return to the closet, and they represented the biggest street mobilisations against homophobia outside of the Pride season for over a decade.

This was impressive given that the vigils and the Liverpool demo had been initiated by individuals.

Many of those involved also showed a desire for unity and a mood for radical action. Outside the BBC people joined together chanting, "We are black, white, Asian, Jew and gay." In Liverpool, hundreds, angered at the police decision to take the protest through backstreets, marched into the shopping centre to reclaim their city. Shoppers stopped and clapped and new slogans emerged: "What do we want? LIBERATION! When do we want it? NOW!" All of this is very significant because the LGBT struggle has made its biggest impact when it has been out on the streets, radical and uniting with wider forces.

But a big question rang through all these events – why was this rise in attacks on LGBT people happening now, and what could be done?

A perfect storm

The ongoing inequalities and discrimination faced by LGBT people makes for an unstable situation in which we are always under threat of attack. But we now face a new element in the situation that is intensifying that threat – a global crisis in capitalism. This may have started with a financial crash but already it has led to people losing their jobs and homes in every major city in the country. This has hit some of the most vulnerable in society hardest with almost half of young black people unemployed. But the worst is yet to come, with two successive governments which have spent over a trillion pounds bailing out the bankers telling us to accept more job cuts and severe attacks on public services.

The scale of the crisis is generating fantastic levels of insecurity among millions about what the future holds along with bitterness, even rage, towards a political system complicit in

THE RED IN THE RAINBOW

the scandals of MPs' expenses, bankers' bonuses and illegal wars. It makes for a volatile situation and creates the potential for resistance, but also for reaction. The YouTube footage from 2009 of car workers in Cowley throwing fruit at their union leaders in fury at being told nothing could be done to save their jobs is symbolic of the way anger does not automatically lead to a fight. The danger of that frustration sliding to the right can be seen in workers' demonstrations for "British jobs for British workers", the anti-Muslim riots and demonstrations organised by the English Defence League (EDL) in towns and cities around the country, and the growth of the BNP. But there have been some important sparks of resistance marked by workers organising occupations and sit-ins, walkouts and all-out strikes against cuts which have won small but significant victories.

The spike in attacks against LGBT people last autumn needs to be understood against this broader picture of polarisation taking place across society between despair and resistance. What course things take from here will be fundamental in shaping the position of LGBT people in society.

No turning back

Every previous crisis has seen the ruling class reach out for a set of ideas which helps to limit our resistance by dividing our side. Sections of the establishment have talked about the need for a "new Thatcher" to deal with the crisis. Commentators like *Financial Times* journalist Martin Wolf, for example, have proposed:

> a sustained freeze on the pay bill; decentralised pay bargaining; employee contributions to public pensions; and a pruning of benefits. The bulk of the action will have to come from control over public spending. The next prime minister is likely to end up quite as hated as Margaret Thatcher was. But, as

she liked to say, there is no alternative. The unsustainable cannot endure. If UK policymakers do not take the needed decisions willingly, markets will force them upon them.[165]

But the fact that the electorate failed to return an overall majority to any party in the 2010 election is a reflection of how far recent events have weakened the credibility of MPs and the political establishment in general. Labour paid the ultimate price and was kicked out of office, but the Tories' failure to capitalise on the deep bitterness generated by Labour's 13 years in government shows there is no appetite for a return to the party of Thatcher. This is why so many people are furious at the Liberal Democrats for joining with the Tories in a "Con-Dem" coalition government. It means such a government will be unlikely to conjure up a new Thatcher. Bank of England chief Mervyn King suggests the government implementing the cuts will be exiled from power for a generation.

But a weak government can also be a nasty one and we should remember how Thatcher tried to drive through a central agenda of attacking the working class by cementing people to imagined communities of nation and family and invoking a series of enemies within including single parents, immigrants and lesbians and gays as well as union power.

At the moment there appears to be a formal consensus among the mainstream parties that is supportive of LGBT equality. Cameron, for example, has made real efforts to rehabilitate the Tories as a gay-friendly party saying, "I think we can look gay people in the eye…because we now support gay equality," and has pledged to review the ban on gay men donating blood. But the *Pink News* poll showing that less than 6 percent of LGBT people would vote Tory shows how few people trust them – and rightly so.[166] Cameron's own record includes voting against adoption rights for gay couples in 2002, against scrapping Section 28 in 2004 and against enabling lesbians to get IVF treatment in 2008. He has also forged a coalition in Europe with the Polish Law and Justice Party whose leader claims "the human race would disappear if homosexuality was freely promoted" encouraging its MPs to attack gays as "faggots" and "positive paedophiles".

The decision of the Liberal Democrats to go into government with a party that its leader Nick Clegg once attacked for its links with "homophobes and nutters" does not offer much hope that they will be principled in support of LGBT rights either. Their failure to protest at the appointment of bigots to key government positions and their backtracking on "illegal" immigrants who they had said should be offered an amnesty only to later support a Tory cap on all migrants are further confirmation of this.

This does not necessarily mean that we will see an attempt to turn the clock back on LGBT rights, since homophobic bigotry is generally very unpopular with voters. But it is likely that appeals to the "national interest" and traditional family values will remain central to the rhetoric of this coalition government. The huge attacks on the welfare state that are to come will also place real burdens on working class families and will require a major bolstering of the idea of family duties and responsibilities.

We have already seen the way in which the policies and language of those in power have encouraged attacks on other oppressed groups. The rhetoric of Britishness and the demonisation of Islam which accompanied the "war on terror" has been combined with crude nationalist responses to the economic crisis, such as the demand for "British jobs", all of which intensify racism towards Muslims and victimise immigrants. These groups are undoubtedly suffering the brunt of attacks at the moment.

This is something we must take a stand against and we will do that more effectively if we understand the dangerous logic of scapegoating, which can be extended to all kinds of groups in society including LGBT people.

The most alarming signal of this has been the growth of the BNP. They have attempted to disguise their core fascist beliefs by donning suits and wrapping their ideas of race in talk of British "identity". But the actions and statements of leading BNP members should leave no doubt that it stands in the tradition of Hitler's Nazi Party which murdered hundreds of thousands of lesbians and gays alongside socialists, gypsies, trade unionists and six million Jews.

BNP members have also played a central role in the EDL, a hard core racist organisation supported by football hooligans and, by the EDL's own admission, "the National Front, Blood And Honour, Combat 18, British Freedom Fighters and other affiliated yet 'autonomous' Nationalistic racist groups".[167] They have organised numerous anti-Muslim demonstrations in towns and cities across Britain that have involved violent physical attacks on sections of the local Asian community as well as assaults on gay areas.

The BNP and EDL are dangerous, precisely because they are feeding off racism promoted by the ruling class against a backdrop of an economic crisis and historic levels of alienation from the political system. In order to defeat them, and the divisive politics being peddled by the mainstream parties, we will need to develop the kind of movement that builds on a spirit and unity of the demonstrations in Liverpool and outside the BBC.

The question of unity against a common enemy is important. The EDL for example has set up an "LGBT division" which claims to defend gays against Muslim homophobia. The idea that Muslims are uniquely homophobic is something that has been encouraged by the general Islamophobia peddled by the establishment. Not only is this a dangerous lie used to beat one of the most oppressed groups in society, but it will ultimately be turned on the rest of us if we don't stand up to it. Hitler's Nazi Party initially had openly gay members in its ranks, but that did not stop it from conducting the most crushing and dramatic reversal in the fortunes of LGBT people who were driven from the gay centre of Weimar Germany to the Nazi death camps.

We must also fight to reclaim the mobilisations that already exist – the seasonal Prides – for the purpose they were originally intended. This requires challenging their treatment as corporate events which are a no-go zone for politics and using them to build and strengthen a movement capable of resisting LGBT oppression and building solidarity with other struggles.

LGBT history month can be used in a similar way to challenge homophobia and transphobia in schools and workplaces across the country and open a discussion about how we unite to fight against it. The positive impact this can have is described by a school teacher in north London who used LGBT history month to take on homophobia in her school. She explains:

The month [LGBT history month] was celebrated in each subject. In science classes, students discussed the "gay gene", in humanities, the treatment of gay people in concentration camps, in technology, the rainbow flag and its meanings. The final whole school assembly began by me asking what does "L" stand for? A resounding "lesbian" was shouted by 1,300 students. The highlight and finale was a gay but not "out" student who had the confidence and determination to sing "An Easier Affair" – a George Michael song about coming out. The best comment came from a year ten boy who stopped me and said he had listened to my assembly. He said he wasn't going to call his friends "gay" any more when they got on his nerves. Instead he would just call them "idiots". I smiled for the rest of the week.[168]

The problem is too few schools attempt this kind of thing

and many head teachers, and employers generally, put up barriers to such initiatives. Very few schools, for example, even carry a single positive image of LGBT people. We need to use the large network that exists among trade unionists and activists to roll out a challenge to institutionalised oppression and bullying. This is important because, in contrast to an equal opportunities box-ticking approach, we can use LGBT history month to engage in a genuine discussion about the need to support each other's struggles, to encourage students to think about why we should unite and to convince trade unionists that LGBT rights are a struggle worth fighting for when so often the law and regulations fail to protect people.

But key to undercutting the politics of divide and rule will be our ability to build the wider struggles to defend our public services, jobs and homes and to fight for more resources. Such resistance is essential if we are going to successfully stop the ruling class assault on our side that is generating many of the divisions, and will help put forward an alternative to blaming each other. The miners' strike did not begin by talking about LGBT liberation but ended up marching in support of it. In the course of that dispute many people began to connect their strike for jobs to the fight against a wider set of injustices in society. The experience of struggle was a liberating one that broke down divisions and forged new ways of seeing the world.

There are many other such inspiring and more recent examples.

South Africa – the red in the Rainbow Nation

Many people wonder how South Africa came to be the first government in the world to recognise the rights of LGBT people in its constitution following the defeat of apartheid. Under this brutal all-white regime, homosexuality was punishable by seven years in prison. Interracial marriage and sex outside of marriage was banned and lesbians and gays in the military were forced to undergo electric shock therapy and sex changes. Any group of men caught dancing together or even socialising could also be charged with seeking to "stimulate sexual gratification".[169]

It took a massive fight to overthrow apartheid. But in the end the mass strikes, demonstrations and uprisings which united students and workers, the townships, churches and unemployed, brought South Africa to the brink of revolution forcing the regime to agree to elections and a political settlement before they were overthrown. In the course of that struggle people helped to transform the position of LGBT people in South Africa and achieved some of the best legislation in the world:

> The mass movement that got rid of apartheid carried with it a vision of a different society. The constitution signed in 1996 symbolised the hopes of millions. Containing the most advanced Bill of Rights in the world it is no surprise that LGBT activists and human rights campaigners celebrated it. We felt that everything was possible: the world was at our feet ready for the taking... For gay and lesbian people this went beyond legislative change, sweeping away generations of shame, discrimination and exclusion.[170]

The relationship between the anti-apartheid and LGBT struggles was one that had to be forged through fighting back and was the source of disagreement and controversy among activists. The largest and predominantly white LGBT organisation, the Gay Association of South Africa (GASA), disgracefully refused to take a position on apartheid. By the mid to late 1980s a number of new LGBT organisations were launched in the wake of revolts in the townships and an increasingly powerful working class movement. These took a commitment to the anti-apartheid struggle as their starting point and actively linked the two struggles through a series of campaigns. They did so in the context of a number of leading figures in the anti-apartheid movement coming out, including Simon Nkoli, who revealed his sexuality while in prison on trumped-up charges designed to undermine the momentum of the struggle. These developments were not embraced by everyone. LGBT activists who came out faced homophobia and arguments claiming that challenging sexual oppression was a diversion from the real struggle.[171] But the combination of a mass movement that saw millions rise against centuries of deep oppression and racism, combined with the work of activists immersed in that movement, was key to transforming the situation for LGBT people in South Africa.

It can be no coincidence that the first lesbian and gay Pride in South Africa took place in 1990 – the same year that Mandela was released from prison and the ANC was decriminalised. Since then Pride in Cape Town has grown from several hundred to tens of thousands and in a number of major cities it is possible to be out and proud.

Events in South Africa provide a powerful illustration of the transformative power of mass struggle – even in the most difficult situation. A key ingredient in that struggle was the growing strength of a working class that was able to paralyse whole sections of the economy with powerful strikes. Few anticipated that this power would end up not only defeating the systematic divisions of race, but also begin to liberate sexuality. It also shows how important it is that LGBT activists don't cut themselves off from the wider struggles taking place. The position that GASA took not only made it irrelevant to the anti-apartheid struggle, but to the sexual liberation struggle too.

These lessons are important not only for the struggle in Britain, but internationally.

Internationalism and the struggle for liberation

Eighty countries still criminalise homosexuality with at least ten carrying the death penalty. Although there have been important gains in the last few years including the repeal of anti-sodomy laws in India dating from the British Empire, we have also seen setbacks and resistance to newly emerging LGBT organisation. In the US gay marriage has been revoked in California. In a number of Eastern European countries attempts to hold Prides and other LGBT public mobilisations have been met with bans and police repression. In Uganda a parliamentary bill is being debated which would introduce the death penalty for homosexuality and criminalise friends and family of lesbians and gays.

But in recent years it is the Middle East that has been singled out as uniquely oppressive. Certainly there is severe repression, including the death penalty, in a number of countries. However, as with anywhere else in the world, the situation, both historically and today, is quite varied and certainly not uniformly oppressive.

It is worth remembering that at a time when the Victorians were imposing new sexual oppressions in the west, the Middle East was seen as a place where one could find sexual experiences unobtainable in Europe. This was something thoroughly exploited by colonialists who took advantage of this greater openness, at the same time as presenting the region as untamed, primitive and a threat to the west in need of "civilisation". The introduction of repressive sodomy laws occurred not in a free, sovereign Middle East or under Islamic rule but under British, French and Italian colonial rule. Since this period, the legacy of colonialism and ongoing imperialist intervention continues to shape the region's laws on sex and sexuality. In the five Arab countries where the death penalty exists for sodomy, three had anti-sodomy laws introduced under British rule: Sudan, Yemen and the United

Arab Emirates.[172]

But it is also misleading to read the situation simply by looking at the legal position. How and when these restrictions on sexuality are implemented is uneven, and often driven by political and economic factors. The beginning of the war on terror, for example, was accompanied by a rise in moral panics against sexual minorities in a number of countries whose governments were complicit in the wars in Afghanistan and Iraq. They sought a superficial means of attacking the West at a time when they were supporting wars that were extremely unpopular with their local populations. In Egypt this also coincided with an economic crisis and attacks on homosexuals offered a very useful means of shoring up the regime's support.

> In the Middle East...attitudes towards homosexuality (along with women's and human rights in general) have become entangled in international politics... Cultural protectionism is one way of opposing Western policies that are viewed as domineering, imperialistic, etc, and so exaggerated images of a licentious West, characterised in the popular imagination by female nudity and male homosexuality, are countered by invoking a supposedly traditional Arab morality.[173]

But many people in the Middle East defy these versions of morality, including in countries where the death penalty exists. In Iran, for example, there are known cruising areas and places where gays hang out. Activists say the Iranian government is wary of intervening for fear of drawing attention to homosexuality and sparking public debate on the question.[174] In Saudi Arabia, where any public display of sexuality is restricted, there are a range of places where gay men can meet each other from shopping malls to cafes and private parties. One anonymous gay man talks about his discovery of:

this whole underground sort of thing… Parties every weekend, where you could feel absolutely free to do anything you've always fantasised about doing in public. Dancing with people of the same sex, kissing, hugging, flirting and looking at people you're attracted to without having to worry if someone is watching you in disgust… Sometimes you even run into people that you know from school or work, or people that you notice in the mall. The people that you would never expect to harbour the same sexual tendencies as you.[175]

Public physical contact between men is also considered much more socially acceptable compared to Britain, enabling gay men to find inventive ways of being "out": "These days… gay men can be out in the way they dress. If I wear a tight or flashy T-shirt straight men just think I am trying to show off…but other gay men know".[176] In the segregated schools of both sexes same-sex relations are also not uncommon.

So when it comes to sexual politics the Middle East is not a monolith. It is a region of many contested spaces *and* there is a struggle taking place.

Learning to dream together

In Lebanon the first gay organisation in the Middle East, Helem (Dream), chose to screen the 1961 British law reform film *Victim* at one of their opening events. This indicates circumstances that are more akin to 1950s Britain than anything; "unnatural intercourse" is a criminal offence but there are also a number of thriving gay areas, particularly in the Shia areas.

Helem was launched in 2001 in the wake of the Queen Boat scandal – a major raid on one of Egypt's gay night clubs on the Nile which saw 52 men arrested, over half locked up, and a hysterical moral panic against homosexuality. Newspaper headlines read "Perverts declare war on Egypt".

This was part of rising government harassment of lesbians and gays in the region, which both Amnesty and Human Rights Watch noted had increased sharply since the war on terror began.

Leading Helem activist Ghassan Makarem argues that against this background the involvement of its activists in the emerging anti-war movement was vital in "winning legitimacy without being accused of being agents of imperialism because of the baseless way human rights and democracy have been used".[177] It also put Helem at the centre of a wider movement from the beginning. Issues of solidarity with Iraq were linked to the struggle for civil and democratic rights. During 2003, a day of massive global anti-war demonstrations saw the rainbow flag raised by gay men for the first time on a public mobilisation in Lebanon. Helem activists wore T-shirts that said "Exist" and badges saying "Indi helem" – echoing Martin Luther King's "I have a dream". Ghassan Makarem explains:

> When we did this it was not that we were particularly accepted in Lebanese society but we were able to create a space that projects itself by being involved in other groups, by having people from other organisations and being visible.[178]

In 2006, when Israel invaded Lebanon, Helem once again put efforts to respond to a war situation at the forefront of their work by opening up their offices as an aid centre for refugees and relief workers. In the context of a devastating war, they worked alongside religious and other groups to provide relief to people whose homes, lives and loved ones were being destroyed by Israeli missiles. People pulled together, relationships were built and the visible involvement of Helem as a gay rights group won them respect from unexpected quarters. Hezbollah unofficially congratulated Helem for their relief work, and the Free Patriot Movement gave them an honorary award for the role they played. During this time Helem also joined the international boycott of World Pride which held some of its activities in Jerusalem during the assault:

> Israel promotes itself as a haven for sexual minorities, as more civilised, then it destroys Lebanese cities and towns... Listening to Western activists speak about Islamofascism and in the same breath justify holding World Pride in occupied Jerusalem should be a clear indicator. The apartheid wall alone makes a mockery of pride's slogan "Love Without Borders".

The process of engaging in struggles against war and invasion has been vital in connecting Helem with a wider network of activists and winning respect, including from groups often dismissed in the West as uniquely homophobic.

The experience is important if we are to understand how we can most effectively give solidarity to people organising in other parts of the world.

First and foremost we have to fight for people to be free to wage their own struggles free from imperialist intervention. That means our home government has to be the main target. There are a number of things we can do to challenge the ongoing British interference in other parts of the world. We should fight to stop the arms and financial aid to regimes like Egypt and Saudi Arabia. We can get involved in resisting wars such as that waged on Iraq, which has devastated the entire country, killed over one million people and opened up a killing spree against gays by death squads, where once there existed some space for lesbians and gays. And we must insist on the right of LGBT refugees to asylum free from persecution by a British government which is happy to send them back, possibly to their deaths. In 2003 an Iranian gay man poured petrol on himself and set himself alight after being refused asylum in Britain.[179] We have to organise to make sure no one is ever forced into this kind of action again.

Success in any of these struggles would surely have a huge impact on the lives of everyone in those countries, LGBT or otherwise. And as we saw in Lebanon, the process of building them can be part of creating a real space where dialogue and debate about sexual liberation can take place. The stop the war movement in Britain, for example, was crucial to the call for a global day of action against the war during which Helem activists unfurled their rainbow banner. The international movement also played an important role in building solidarity with the anti-apartheid struggle in South Africa.

But it cannot be for activists in countries like Britain, with its long history of imperialist aggression and racism, to think we can lead struggles on behalf of people in other parts of the world. That kind of approach can often make it harder for activists on the ground in other countries to build the kind of resistance and alliances necessary to win fundamental change. If you are based in Zimbabwe, for example, where President Robert Mugabe denounces homosexuality as "un-African", it does not help for any campaign to be led by people based in Britain – the country most implicated in the colonial and racist oppression of that country. Rather we can help to inspire resistance internationally by building examples of resistance here, as well as responding to calls for solidarity and sensitively debating ideas about the best way to take the struggle forward.

What kind of change are we fighting for?

LGBT struggle can only be waged effectively if it is linked to the wider issues that shape our age. These kinds of struggles have been central to winning the gains we enjoy today. But we will have to go further if we are to achieve liberation.

In South Africa, for example, some of the remarkable gains made for LGBT people in the course of the anti-apartheid struggle have suffered serious setbacks. The constitutional rights to equality and dignity remain in place, but there has been a worrying rise in violence against LGBT people. Thirty one lesbians have been reported murdered since 1998 and there has been a chilling increase in "corrective rapes" against lesbians, supposedly aimed at "curing" them, in cities like Cape Town and Johannesburg.[180] Human rights organisations have put these developments down to extreme frustration caused by poverty and unemployment in a country where many people do not even have access to clean water and electricity and over five million are suffering from HIV/AIDS. The struggle that was waged against apartheid had those in power fearful of revolution. But in the end a new world was not born. Apartheid was dismantled but capitalism remained, and the new government has embraced a system that has continued to generate poverty and misery for the majority.

The situation in South Africa reminds us that unless we achieve a more complete transformation of the system even the gains of the most inspiring struggle will be limited.

That is why the highpoints of the struggle for sexual liberation have taken place whenever our struggles have flowed together in ways that present a more fundamental challenge to capitalism. The impact of the Stonewall riots, and the movement they gave birth to, was shaped by a global revolt involving mass movements and strikes that were bringing governments to their knees. As the slogan "All power to the imagination" reverberated through mass strikes in France, heralding the possibility of revolution in the advanced capitalist world, people felt confident and inspired to put forward a vision of sexual liberation that was about "tearing down the walls in which sexist society has chained us" and to rebel against all the restrictions imposed by capitalism on our sexuality. As the GLF's manifesto declared:

> We are a revolutionary group of men and women formed with the realisation that complete sexual liberation for all people cannot come about unless existing social institutions are abolished. We reject society's attempt to impose sexual roles and definitions of our nature. We are stepping outside these roles and simplistic myths. We are going to be who we are. At the same time, we are creating new social forms and relations based upon brotherhood, cooperation, human love and uninhibited sexuality... Gay liberation doesn't just mean reforms. It means a revolutionary change in our whole society.[181]

Perhaps the most powerful illustration of this is the Russian Revolution. In the course of that revolution people used their power to go beyond just challenging capitalism and started to build a different kind of society, socialism, that sought to bring about liberation for all. Despite the enormously difficult circumstances of poverty and civil war, and despite the absence of a gay movement, they made huge gains for sexual liberation. Homosexuality was decriminalised and an end to the interference of the state, religion and the market in sexual affairs was declared. But fundamental to the revolution were the attempts to build a material basis for those declarations by mobilising society's resources to give people real control over their lives, from the workplace to their most intimate relationships. A revolution that demanded "peace, bread and land" took the position of women as the "yardstick" of its progress and transformed the most personal aspects of people's lives, such that a drag queen in Kursk could interpret the revolution "as a licence to be quite flagrant and outrageous" and a marriage between two women was recognised.

This is one glimpse of the powerful potential of revolution to open up new possibilities and freedoms in people's personal and sexual lives. As Engels once argued:

> What we can now conjecture about the way in which sexual relations will be ordered after the…overthrow of capitalist production is mainly of a negative character, limited for the most part to what will disappear. But what will there be new? That will be answered when a new generation has grown up: a generation of men who never in their lives have known what it is to buy a woman's surrender with money or any other instrument of power. A generation of women who have never known what it is to give themselves to a man from any other considerations than real love… When these people are in the world, they will care precious little about what anybody thinks they ought to do; they will make their own practice and their corresponding public opinion about the practice of each individual – and that will be the end of it.[182]

The history of our struggle for sexual freedom has shown no shortage of activists and movements prepared to take a stand against oppression. Today we must take into such struggles a vision of tomorrow that does not accept that this is as good as it gets. Oscar Wilde once said, "A map of the world that does not include utopia is not worth even glancing at." We must use our resistance to shape a world where people can express their sexuality and gender identity without fear or persecution – a socialist world where we win liberation for all.

Notes

1   2005 Whitehall figures compiled while analysing the financial
    implications of the Civil Partnerships Act.

2   See the National Survey of Sexual Attitudes and Lifestyles, 1989/90
    and 1999/2000 and "Sex Uncovered", *The Observer*, 26 October
    2008.

3   For a range of interesting research and statistics on sexual
    behaviours and attitudes see http://en.wikipedia.org/wiki/
    Homosexuality

4   Alfred Kinsey, *Sexual Behaviour in the Human Male and Sexual
    Behaviour in the Human Female* (University of Indiana Press,
    1998), pp610-666 and pp446-510 respectively.

5   As above, pp659-660.

6   As above, pp638-639.

7   Colin Wilson, *Gay Liberation and Socialism* (Bookmarks, 1995),
    p8.

8   Will Roscoe, *Changing Ones: Third and Fourth Genders in Native
    North America* (St Martin's Press, 1998).

9   See Stephen Murray and Will Roscoe (eds), *Boy-Wives and Female
    Husbands: Studies of African Homosexualities* (St Martin's Press,
    1998).

10 Norah Carlin, "The Roots of Gay Oppression", *International
    Socialism* 42 (Spring 1989), p73.

11 See Stephen Murray and Will Roscoe, *Islamic Homosexualities:
    Culture, History and Literature* (New York University Press, 1997).

12 Alan Bray, *The Friend* (University of Chicago Press, 2003),
    pp78-83.

13 Carlin, as above, p73.

14 Frederick Engels, *The Origin of the Family, Private Property and
    the State* (Peking, 1978), p4.

15 Eleanor Burke Leacock, *Myths of Male Dominance* (Haymarket

Books, 2008), p49.

16 As above, p33.

17 As above, p49.

18 Michelle Robidoux, "The Origins of Lesbian and Gay Oppression", unpublished paper.

19 Chris Harman, "Engels and the Origins of Human Society", *International Socialism* 65 (Winter 1994), p121.

20 As above, p139.

21 Engels, as above, pp65-66.

22 As above, p66.

23 Carlin, as above, p72.

24 Louis Crompton, *Homosexuality and Civilization* (Harvard University Press, 2003), p233.

25 Carlin, as above, p77.

26 Gerrard Winstanley of the Diggers quoted in Christopher Hill (ed), *Winstanley: "The Law of Freedom" and Other Writings* (Penguin, 1973), p388.

27 Carlin, as above, p85.

28 As above, p84.

29 Robert Aldrich (ed), *Gay Life and Culture: A World History* (Thames & Hudson, 2006), p120.

30 Colin Wilson, "LGBT Politics and Sexual Liberation", *International Socialism* 114 (Spring 2007), p139.

31 Aldrich, as above, p103.

32 Carlin, as above, p86.

33 Chris Harman, *A People's History of the World* (Bookmarks, 1999), p325.

34 Lindsey German, *Sex, Class and Socialism* (Bookmarks, 1994), p20.

35 Frederick Engels, *The Condition of the Working Class in England*, Marxists Internet Archive, http://www.marxists.org/archive/marx/works/1845/condition-working-class/index.htm

36 As above.

37 Quoted in James Boswell, *The Journal of a Tour to the Hebrides with Samuel Johnson*.

38 David F Greenberg, *The Construction of Homosexuality* (University of Chicago Press, 1988), pp366-367.

39 As above, p58.

40 Engels, *The Condition of the Working Class in England*, as above, p324.

41 Carlin, as above, p88.

42 Jeffrey Weeks, *Sex, Politics and Society: The Regulation of Sexuality since 1800* (Longman, 1989), p100.

43 Charles Upchurch, *Before Wilde: Sex Between Men in Britain's Age of Reform* (University of California Press, 2009).

44 As above, p92.

45 Audrey Farrell, *Crime, Class and Corruption: The Politics of the Police* (Bookmarks, 1992), p53.

46 Upchurch, as above, pp50-79.

47 Harman, *A People's History of the World*, as above, pp324-325.

48 Carlin, as above, p91.

49 Dorothy Thompson, "Women and Nineteenth Century Radical Politics", in Juliet Mitchell and Ann Oakley (eds), *The Rights and Wrongs of Women* (Penguin, 1977), p129.

50 Karl Marx, *The German Ideology*, http://www.marxists.org/archive/marx/works/1845/german-ideology/ch01d.htm

51 Judith Walkowitz, *Prostitution and Victorian Society: Women, Class and the State* (Cambridge University Press, 1980), p5.

52 Quoted from *The Sentinel* (1885) in Jeffrey Weeks, *Coming Out* (BPCC Hazel Books, 1990), p18.

53 Weeks, *Coming Out*, as above, p20.

54 As above, p16.

55 Weeks, *Sex, Politics and Society*, as above, p103.

56 Noel Halifax, *Out, Proud and Fighting: Gay Liberation and the Struggle for Socialism* (SWP, 1988), p15.

57 John Steakley, *The Homosexual Emancipation Movement in Germany* (Arno Press, 1975), p15.

58 As above, p27.

59 John Lauritsen and David Thorstad, *The Early Homosexual Rights Movement (1864-1935)* (Times Change Press, 1974), p58.

60 Wilson, *Gay Liberation and Socialism*, as above, pp14-15.

61 See for example Harry Oosterhuis, *Stepchildren of Nature: Krafft-Ebing, Psychiatry, and the Making of Sexual Identity* (University of Chicago Press, 2000).

62 Lauritsen and Thorstad, as above, p22.

63 As above, p32.

64 Steakley, as above, p32.

65 As above, p28.

66 Hal Draper, *The Two Souls of Socialism* (Bookmarks, 1996).

67 Halifax, as above, p15.

68 Lauritsen and Thorstad, as above, p26.

69 Chris Harman, *The Lost Revolution: Germany 1918-1923* (Bookmarks, 1997), p26.

70 Lauritsen and Thorstad, as above, p63.

71 Leon Trotsky, *Women and the Family* (Pathfinder Press, 1974), p23.

72 *Alexandra Kollontai on Women's Liberation* (Bookmarks, 1998).

73 As above, p25.

74 Dan Healey, *Homosexual Desire in Revolutionary Russia: The Regulation of Sexual and Gender Dissent* (University of Chicago Press, 2001), p111.

75 Quoted in Colin Wilson, "Sexual Liberation and the Russian Revolution", *Socialist Worker*, 20 January 2007.

76 Healey, as above, p70.

77 Lauritsen and Thorstad, as above, p67.

78 Trotsky, as above, p37.

79 Kollontai, as above, p28.

80 Harman, *A People's History of the World*, as above, p434.

81 Steakley, as above, p81.

82 Lauritsen and Thorstad, as above, p27.

83 Steakley, as above, p30.

84 Lauritsen and Thorstad, as above, p30.

85 Neil Miller, *Out of the Past: Gay and Lesbian History from 1869 to the Present* (Vintage, 1995), p124.

86 Steakley, as above, p72.

87 As above, p82.

88 As above, p72.

89 As above, p40.

90 Harman, *A People's History of the World*, as above, p470.

91 As above, p483.

92 Steakley, as above, p118.

93 James D Steakley, "Homosexuals and the Third Reich", *The Body Politic* 11 (January/February 1974), http://www.fordham.edu/halsall/pwh/steakley-nazis.html

94 V I Lenin, *Collected Works*, vol 32 (Moscow, 1965), p24.

95 Leon Trotsky, *The Revolution Betrayed* (New Park, 1973), p112.

96 Harman, *A People's History of the World*, as above, p474.

97 Victor Serge, *From Lenin to Stalin* (1937), http://www.marxists.org/archive/serge/index.htm

98 John D'Emilio, *Sexual Politics, Sexual Identities* (University of Chicago Press, 1983), p232.

99 Donn Teal, *The Gay Militants: How Gay Liberation Began in America, 1969-1971* (St Martin's Press, 1971), p7.

100 Jeffrey Weeks, *Coming Out*, as above, p188.

101 D'Emilio, as above, p50.

102 David Eisenbach, *Gay Power: An American Revolution* (Carroll and Garf, 2006), p81.

103 Weeks, *Coming Out*, as above, p164.

104 D'Emilio, as above, p63.

105 As above, p66.

106 As above, p81.

107 As above, p117.

108 Sara Evans, *Personal Politics: The Roots of Women's Liberation in the Civil Rights Movement and the New Left* (Vintage, 1980), p3.

109 D'Emilio, as above, p153.

110 Eisenbach, as above, p108.

111 Gay Liberation Front Manifesto, 1971.

112 Shulamith Firestone, *The Dialectic of Sex* (1970), http://www.marxists.org/subject/women/authors/firestone-shulamith/dialectic-sex.htm

113 Lindsey German, "The Rise and Fall of the Women's Movement", *International Socialism* 37 (Winter 1988), pp9-10.

114 Radicalesbians, *The Woman-Identified Woman* (1970), http://scriptorium.lib.duke.edu/wlm/womid/

115 *Gay Left: A Socialist Journal produced by Gay People*, number 2 (Spring 1976), p1.

111 Mike Jackson, *Fucking with Miners: The Story of Lesbians and Gays Support the Miners*, p10.

117 As above, p7.

118 As above, p10.

119 David Donovan from the Dulais mining community, December 1984, quoted in Mike Jackson, as above, p1.

120 Weeks, *Coming Out*, as above, p239.

121 Margaret Thatcher interviewed by Douglas Keay for *Woman's Own*, 31 October 1987, http://www.margaretthatcher.org/speeches/displaydocument.asp?docid=106689

122 See Peter Tatchell, *The Battle for Bermondsey* (Gay Men's Press, 1983).

123 Halifax, *Out, Proud and Fighting*, as above, p35.

124 Jeffrey Weeks, *Sexuality and its Discontents* (Routledge, 1990).

125 Eisenbach, as above, p308.

126 Jonathan Neale, "The Politics of AIDS", *International Socialism* 53 (Winter 1991).

127 Eisenbach, as above, p292.

128 As above, p300.

129 Dennis Altman, *The Homosexualization of America* (St Martin's Press, 1982).

130 Weeks, *Coming Out*, as above, pp244-245.

131 Eisenbach, as above, p300.

132 Matt Cook, *A Gay History of Britain* (Greenwood World Publishing, 2007), p205.

133 As above, p206.

134 Conservative Family Campaign, "HIV Infected Citizens: Charter of Responsibility" (27 September 1991).

135 Weeks, *Coming Out*, as above, p244.

136 www.stonewall.org.uk/about_us/2532.asp

137 www.stonewall.org.uk/about_us/2532.asp

138 www.stonewall.org.uk/documents/accounts_0405.pdf

139 "QUEERS READ THIS", leaflet distributed at Pride march in New York, published anonymously by Queers (June, 1990), http://www.qrd.org/qrd/misc/text/queers.read.this

140 Interview in *Outlines*, October 1990.

141 "QUEERS READ THIS", as above.

142 Nicola Field, *Over the Rainbow* (Pluto Press, 1995), p52.

143 Jeffrey Escoffier, "Socialism as Ethics" in Socialist Review Collective (eds), *Unfinished Business: 20 Years of Socialist Review* (London, 1991), p319.

144 Interview with Judith Butler by Regina Michalik (LOLApress), May 2001, http://lolapress.org/elec2/artenglish/butl_e.htm

145 Judith Butler, *Gender Trouble: Feminism and the Subversion of Identity* (Routledge, 1990), p5.

146 Peter Mandelson and Roger Liddle, *The Blair Revolution* (Faber and Faber, 1996), p1.

147 Hugh Muir, *The Guardian*, 23 May 2007.

148 BBC News, 5 December 2005.

149 Jeffrey Weeks, *The World We Have Won* (Routledge, 2007), p103.

150 Office for National Statistics (ONS), *Popular Trends* (2009), http://www.statistics.gov.uk/downloads/theme_population/Popular-Trends136.pdf

151 As above.

152 Lindsey German, *Material Girls: Women, Men and Work* (Bookmarks, 2007).

153 ONS figures up to end of 2007, http://www.statistics.gov.uk/cci/nugget.asp?id=1685

154 Fleishman-Hillard, http://www.fleishmanhillard.com/

155 *CNN Money*, 25 April 2006, http://money.cnn.com/2006/04/25/magazines/fortune/pluggedin_fortune/index.htm

156 Ruth Hunt and Johan Jensen, *The School Report: The Experiences of Young Gay People in Britain's Schools* (Stonewall,

2007), http://www.stonewall.org.uk/at_school/resources/3778.asp

157 Peter Kelley and Susan Paterson, *Filling in the Blanks: LGBT Hate Crime in London* (Galop, 2009), p70.

158 Sam Dick, *Homophobic Hate Crime: The Gay British Crime Survey* (Stonewall, 2008), www.stonewall.org.uk/documents/homophobic_hate_crime__final_report.pdf

159 As above.

160 TUC, *Straight Up! Why the Law should Protect Lesbian and Gay Workers* (TUC, 2000).

161 Katherine Cowan and Gill Valentine, *Tuned Out: The BBC's Portrayal of Lesbian and Gay People* (Stonewall, 2006), http://www.stonewall.org.uk/documents/tuned_out_pdf_1.pdf

162 Ben Summerskill (ed), *The Way We Are Now, Gay and Lesbian Lives in the 21st Century* (Continuum, 2005).

163 Karen McVeigh, "Gay Community Split Over 'Depoliticised' London Pride", *The Guardian*, 4 July 2009.

164 Johann Hari, "Violence Against Gay People Can and Must be Stopped", *The Independent*, 4 November 2009.

165 Martin Wolf, *Financial Times*, 7 May 2009.

166 "PinkNews.co.uk poll finds Tory support among gays drops below the Green Party", 4 May 2010, www.pinknews.co.uk/2010/05/04/pinknews.co.uk-poll-finds-tory-vote-drops-further

167 Tommy Robinson (not his real name), the spokesperson for the EDL quoted in Martin Smith, *Socialist Review* (May 2010).

168 Elly Barnes, "LGBT History Month was Life Changing in my School", *Socialist Worker*, 17 March 2008.

169 Neville Hoad, Karen Martin and Graeme Reid (eds), *Sex and Politics in South Africa* (Double Storey Books, 2005).

170 Viv Smith, "The Rainbow Nation Today", *Socialist Review* (February 2008).

171 Leading ANC member Ruth Mompati: "We don't have a policy on gays and lesbians. We don't have a policy on flower sellers either," quoted in *Capital Gay*, 18 September 1987.

172 Brian Whitaker, *Unspeakable Love: Gay and Lesbian Life in the Middle East* (Saqi Books, 2006), p123.

173 As above, p11.

174 *Inside Iran's Secret Gay World*, documentary available on YouTube.

175 Whitaker, as above, p55.

176 As above, p54.

177 Ghassan Makarem speaking at Marxism 2006, London, on how to fight for LGBT liberation in the Middle East.

178 As above.

179 Wilson, "LGBT Politics and Sexual Liberation", as above, p159.

180 http://www.guardian.co.uk/world/2009/mar/12/eudy-simelane-corrective-rape-south-africa

181 D'Emilio, as above, p234.

182 Engels, *The Origin of the Family*, as above, p96.

Index

THE RED IN THE RAINBOW

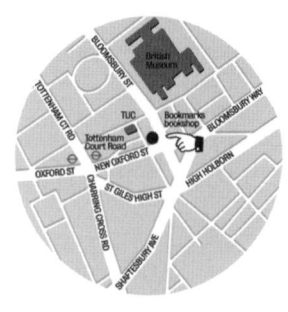